101 POEMS BY 101 WOMEN

by the same author

THE FEMALE EUNUCH
THE OBSTACLE RACE:
The Fortunes of Women Painters and Their Work
SEX AND DESTINY:
The Politics of Human Fertility
THE MADWOMAN'S UNDERCLOTHES
SHAKESPEARE
DADDY, WE HARDLY KNEW YOU
THE CHANGE:
Women, Ageing and the Menopause
SLIP-SHOD SIBYLS:
Recognition, Rejection and the Woman Poet
THE WHOLE WOMAN
JOHN WILMOT, EARL OF ROCHESTER

101 POEMS BY 101 WOMEN

edited by
GERMAINE GREER

faber and faber

First published in 2001
by Faber and Faber Limited
3 Queen Square London WC1N 3AU

Photoset by Wilmaset Ltd, Wirral
Printed in Italy

A CIP record for this book
is available from the British Library

ISBN 0–571–20734–0

2 4 6 8 10 9 7 5 3 1

Contents

To the Reader

Within the covers of this small book every reader will find something to deplore. Those who disapprove of the very idea of a collection of poems exclusively by women will be ready to declare the enterprise despicable without reading a single poem, let alone the whole salmagundi. Laura Riding, Kathleen Raine and Elizabeth Bishop all refused in their time to appear in sex-segregated collections. They would have let their works appear in an anthology representing a decade or a nationality or a school or a genre, but not a sex. They would rather have been forgotten than remembered only as women poets. This posture implies a contempt for 'women's poetry' as essentially inferior (an essentialist position in itself). Men have written more feeble, sentimental, insipid, jingoistic, pious and puerile verse than women have and some women have been rewarded far more richly than men for doing the same. L.E.L. and Felicia Hemans were both more successful than their male contemporaries, but their fame did not outlive their generation. There was no conspiracy to bury them; they were simply overwhelmed. The same fate may have already befallen Laura Riding, Kathleen Raine and Anne Ridler, all of whom were celebrated by their generation.

There would be no excuse for presenting this collection of poems if, by doing so, I were to imply that having read these 101 there was no need to read any more, or that this 101 represents the best of which women poets have been capable. The best women's poetry may be still unrecognised if, as I suspect, we have not yet understood how to read it.

What I hope I have done is to have worked a sampler, a selection of odd and interesting morsels, that will whet the appetite for more. I can say with confidence that there is better poetry by women than most of what you will find in this book, but most of it is by Emily Dickinson, and I promised myself that I would introduce you to 101 women, all of whom are worth knowing, for different reasons. Another rule I inflicted on myself and you was that the 101 poems would be poems and not bits of poems; this has resulted in the exclusion of *Goblin Market* and *Aurora Leigh* (both masterpieces) as miles too long to quote in full, and the reprinting of other poems entire, longueurs and all. The strongest four stanzas of Fanny Greville's 'Prayer for Indifference' are regularly anthologised; as they hang in the whole poem like a bumble-bee in a spider-web, the effect is worth perusal. Amy Lowell's 'The Sisters' is remarkable for its garrulity, as well as the refashioning of the likenesses of Sappho, Elizabeth Barrett Browning and Emily Dickinson, none of whom was as staid as she herself.

Some of the poetry I have chosen is frankly bad; all of it is imperfect. My main criterion has been the only one that interested Emily Dickinson, who brushed aside all Higginson's cavils about her syntax and rhyme and asked only whether her poems lived, asked and received no answer. All 101 of these poems have a life of their own; though they may limp or writhe or grunt instead of singing and dancing, shriek and gibber rather than reason and persuade, they are alive.

In all cases the poet writes as a woman, which was another of my criteria. In at least one case the writer might not have actually been a woman; scholars have hunted 'Ephelia' through every nook and cranny of the 1670s and cannot find her. She may be an extended prank of bored courtiers desperate to while away the long hours in the presence chambers at Whitehall. If she is, she performs womanhood in a new way, refracting the tradition of female complaint until the rejected woman is dancing lop-sidedly in female rage. 'The Ballad of Anne Askew' too might have been written by a committee of propagandists trying to cash in on the conversion potential of Askew's being burnt alive in front of a huge crowd in 1546. Pack-aging of female artists was not invented for the Spice Girls. Many of the women in this book could be considered frauds, but I have included them because in their work they con-front their own lack of authenticity. The ventriloquist's dummy can be heard to speak in her own voice as long as she does not pass herself off as the ventriloquist. L.E.L. could only once have taken off her mask of dazzling virginal brightness to write 'Lines of Life'; now that I know she not only scribbled millions of words for her editor but bore and concealed and was ultimately forced to abandon three ille-gitimate children by him, 'Lines of Life', blunt as it is, cuts deep. Lady Mary Wroth too bore her lover's children as she waited in vain for months on end for him to visit her in the country.

Modernising the poems has brought me hard up against something I already knew, that most of the earlier and some of the later women could, or at any rate did, not write in sen-tences. Clauses, main and subordinate, and phrases adjec-tival and adverbial, occur in any order, are given equal value, and reflect forwards and backwards, leapfrogging over full-stops, swinging themselves along on a chain of 'ands'. Some of the syntactic mayhem is the result of ignor-ance, but more is deliberate. Poetry has its Guerrilla Girls who will snatch up a convention, turn it on its head and bare its nether parts of cliché. It is beyond me to decide how much of the parody of masculine poetry in these pages is innocent and inadvertent, and how much knowing and subversive. It is easier to see how and why Stevie Smith deflates the reader's expectations than to judge the same process of mocking and self-mocking in a poet of the Renaissance.

Poetry is strange stuff and over the centuries it has got stranger. Five hundred or so years ago any gentleman was expected to able to pen on demand a respectable sonnet to his mistress' eyebrow, but by the beginning of the nine-teenth century poetry had been transformed from an elegant accomplishment to a savage destiny, a sacred and sublime vocation, not to be attempted by anyone who shrank at the prospect of madness, destitution and death. Women had struggled to be poets when what was needed was the education that they had not got, and they continued to struggle to be poets when what was demanded was egomania of delusional proportions. Post-modernism has taken some of the pressure off; irony is a medium that women have always understood.

Many of the poems in this sampler are uneven, even crude, but their rawness is sometimes their strength. A woman who speaks firmly, talks loud and draws a crowd, will appear strident to those who think that only men may raise their voices. I don't know whether Maya Angelou really means 'Phenomenal Woman' but the question is worth thinking about. No male poet would stoop to write 'Phenomenal Man'. Poems in praise of the penis do exist, but they have never amounted to a genre. In some cases, as with Anna Wickham and Anne Sexton, I have chosen to side-step exhibitionistic clamour and have opted for something more thoughtful – glimpses of the poet who might have been.

What I have chosen are 101 poems by 101 women, all of them written from the point of view of a woman and most of them about being female. Looking at them as a group, I am startled by the intensity of the anger in them. Poetry and plaint are cognate, but these are not the laments of despoiled maidens so dear to the hearts of our male poets. Even bereavement is here infused with anger. Resignation is explained, justified and enacted in lines of iron that bite into the brain. God has seldom appeared more unjust than he does in Mary Carey's apparently submissive poem on the sight of her aborted foetus. Though in paraphrasing a psalm the Countess of Pembroke was carrying out the most disciplined of devotional exercises, her God is a republican and a subversive.

Some of the poems I have included are obscure, one in fact never before printed, others once only. Others, 'Battle Hymn of the Republic', 'Casabianca' and 'Mary had a little Lamb', for example, are known to everyone. I think it quite proper to remind readers that women poets have been more damaged by celebrity than lack of it (though I drew the line at hymnody). Applause is sustaining only as long as it is merited and comes from people of both sincerity and judgement. Which is not to say that these three poems are bad poems, just because they have been well hackneyed. They are better than they needed to be, and have more life in them than thousands of more pretentious works. With the passage of time their fumbling inexactness may transmute to mystery and incantation. Charisma is much the same in poems as in people.

Germaine Greer
Stump Cross, 2001

101 POEMS BY 101 WOMEN

The Ballad which Anne Askew made and sang when she was in Newgate

Like as the arméd knight
　　Appointed to the field,
With this world will I fight,
　　And faith shall be my shield.

Faith is that weapon strong
　　Which will not fail at need;
My foes therefore among
　　Therewith will I proceed.

As it is had in strength
　　And force of Christ's way,
It will prevail at length,
　　Though all the devils say nay.

Faith in the fathers old
　　Obtainéd righteousness,
Which makes me very bold
　　To fear no world's distress.

I now rejoice in heart,
　　And hope bid me do so,
For Christ will take my part,
　　And ease me of my woe.

Thou sayst, Lord, whoso knock,
　　To them wilt Thou attend;
Undo therefore the lock,
　　And Thy strong power send.

More enemies now I have
    Than hairs upon my head;
Let them not me deprave,
    But fight Thou in my stead.

On Thee my care I cast,
    For all their cruel spite,
I set not by their haste
    For Thou art my delight.

I am not she that list
    My anchor to let fall,
For every drizzling mist,
    My ship substantial.

Not oft use I to write
    In prose nor yet in rhyme,
Yet will I show one sight
    That I saw in my time.

I saw a royal throne
    Where Justice should have sit,
But in her stead was one
    Of moody cruel wit.

Absorbed was righteousness
    As of the raging flood;
Satan in his excess
    Sucked up the guiltless blood.

Then thought I, Jesus, Lord,
    When Thee shalt judge us all,
Hard is it to record
    On these men what will fall.

[4]

Yet, Lord, I Thee desire,
  For that they do to me,
Let them not taste the hire
  Of their iniquity.

  (1546)

To my Friend Master T.L.
whose good nature I see abused

Did not Dame Ceres tell to you
    nor fame unto you show?
What sturdy storms have been abroad
    and who hath played the shrew?
I thought the Goddess in your fields
    had helped you with your crop,
Or else that Fame till you had known,
    her trump would never stop.
But sith I see their silentness,
    I cease the same to write,
Lest I therefore might be condemned
    to do it for a spite.
But this I wish that you, my friend,
    go choose some virtuous wife
With whom in fear of God to spend
    the residue of your life,
For whilst you are in single state
    none hath that right regard.
They think all well that they can win,
    and count it their reward.
With sorrow I too oft have seen,
    when some would fleece you much,
And oft in writing would I say,
    'Good friend beware of such.'
But all my words they were as wind;
    my labour all was spent,
And in the end for my good will
    most cruelly was shent.

If I were boxed and buffeted,
    goodwill shall never cease,
Nor hand, nor tongue, shall so be charmed
    to make me hold my peace.
Wherefore I warn you once again,
    be wary of yourself,
For some have sworn to like you well
    so long as you have pelf.
If warnings still you do reject,
    too late your self shall rue.
Do as you list, I wish you well,
    and so I say adieu.

                    Your wellwiller. Is. W.

(1573)

The doubt of future foes exiles my present joy,
And wit me warns to shun such snares as threaten mine
    annoy,
For falsehood now doth flow, and subject faith doth ebb,
Which would not be, if reason ruled or wisdom weaved the
    web;
But clouds of toys untried do cloak aspiring minds,
Which turn to rain of late repent, by course of changéd
    winds.
The top of hope supposed, the root of ruth will be,
And fruitless all their grafféd guiles, as shortly you shall see.
Then dazzled eyes with pride, which great ambition blinds,
Shall be unsealed by worthy wights, whose foresight
    falsehood finds.
The daughter of debate, that eke discord doth sow,
Shall reap no gain where former rule hath taught still peace
    to grow.
No foreign banished wight shall anchor in this port.
Our realm it brooks no stranger's force; let them elsewhere
    resort.
Our rusty sword with rest shall now his edge employ,
To poll their tops that seek such change and gape for joy.

(1570)

Psalm 82, *Deus stetit*

Where poor men plead at princes' bar,
Who gods, as God's vice-regents, are,
The God of gods hath His tribunal pight,
　　Adjudging right
Both to the judge and judgéd wight.

'How long will ye just doom neglect?
How long,' saith He, 'bad men protect?
You should his own unto the helpless give,
　　The poor relieve,
Ease him with right whom wrong doth grieve.

'You should the fatherless defend;
You should unto the weak extend
Your hand to loose, and quiet his estate,
　　Through lewd men's hate
Entangled now in deep debate.

'This should you do, but what do ye?
You nothing know, you nothing see,
No light, no law. Fie! fie! the very ground
　　Becomes unsound,
So right, wrong, all your faults confound.

'Indeed to you the style I gave
Of gods, and sons of God to have,
But err not Princes, you as men must die.
　　You that sit high
Must fall and low as others lie.'

Since men are such, O God, arise,
Thyself most strong, most just, most wise.

Of all the earth King, Judge, Disposer be,
    Since to decree
Of all the earth belongs to Thee!

*(c.*1600)

The Description of Cookham

Farewell, sweet Cookham, where I first obtained
Grace from that grace where perfect grace remained,
And where the Muses gave their full consent
I should have the power the virtuous to content,
Where princely palace willed me to indite
The sacred story of the soul's delight.
Farewell, sweet place, where virtue then did rest,
And all delights did harbour in her breast.
Never shall my sad eyes again behold
Those pleasures which my thoughts did then unfold;
Yet you, great lady, mistress of that place,
Vouchsafe to think upon those pleasures past
As fleeting worldly joys that could not last,
Or, as dim shadows of celestial pleasures,
Which are desired above all earthly treasures.
Oh how, methought, against you thither came,
Each part did seem some new delight to frame!
The house received all ornaments to grace it,
And would endure no foulness to deface it.
The walks put on their summer liveries,
And all things else did hold like similes:
The trees with leaves, with fruits, with flowers clad,
Embraced each other, seeming to be glad,
Turning themselves to beauteous canopies
To shade the bright sun from your brighter eyes.
The crystal streams, with silver spangles graced
While by the glorious sun they were embraced,
The little birds in chirping notes did sing,
To entertain both you and that sweet spring,

And Philomela with her sundry lays,
Both you and that delightful place did praise.
Oh how, methought, each plant, each flower, each tree
Set forth their beauties then to welcome thee!
The very hills right humbly did descend
When you to tread upon them did intend.
And as you set your feet, they still did rise,
Glad that they could receive so rich a prize.
The gentle winds did take delight to be
Among those woods that were so graced by thee.
And in sad murmur uttered pleasing sound,
That pleasure in that place might more abound:
The swelling banks delivered all their pride,
When such a Phœnix once they had espied.
Each arbour, bank, each seat, each stately tree,
Thought themselves honoured in supporting thee.
The pretty birds would oft come to attend thee,
Yet fly away for fear they should offend thee.
The little creatures in the borough by
Would come abroad to sport them in your eye,
Yet fearful of the bow in your fair hand,
Would run away when you did make a stand.
Now let me come unto that stately tree,
Wherein such goodly prospects you did see,
That oak that did in height his fellows pass,
As much as lofty trees low growing grass,
Much like a comely cedar straight and tall,
Whose beauteous stature far exceeded all.
How often did you visit this fair tree,
Which, seeming joyful in receiving thee,
Would like a palm tree spread his arms abroad,
Desirous that you should there make abode,
Whose fair green leaves much like a comely veil,

Defended Phœbus when he would assail,
Whose pleasing boughs did yield a cool fresh air,
Joying his happiness when you were there,
Where being seated, you might plainly see,
Hills, vales, and woods, as if on bended knee
They had appeared, your honour to salute,
Or to prefer some strange unlooked for suit,
All interlaced with brooks and crystal springs,
A prospect fit to please the eyes of kings,
And thirteen shires appeared all in your sight?
Europe could not afford much more delight.
What was there then but gave you all content,
While you the time in meditation spent,
Of their Creator's power, which there you saw,
In all His creatures held a perfect law;
And in their beauties did you plain descry,
His beauty, wisdom, love and majesty?
In these sweet woods how often did you walk,
With Christ and His Apostles there to talk,
Placing His holy writ in some fair tree,
To meditate what you did therein see?
With Moses you did mount His holy hill,
To know His pleasure and perform His will.
With lovely David you did often sing
His holy hymns to Heaven's eternal King,
And in sweet music did your soul delight,
To sound His praises, morning, noon, and night.
With blessed Joseph you did often feed
Your pinéd brethren, when they stood in need.
And that sweet lady, sprung from Clifford's race,
Of noble Bedford's blood, fair stream of grace,
To honourable Dorset now espoused,
In whose fair breast true virtue then was housed,

Oh what delight did my weak spirits find
In those pure parts of her well-framed mind!
And yet it grieves me that I cannot be
Near unto her, whose virtues did agree
With those fair ornaments of outward beauty,
Which did enforce from all both love and duty.
Unconstant Fortune, thou art most to blame,
Who casts us down into so low a frame,
Where our great friends we cannot daily see,
So great a difference there is in degree.
Many are placéd in those orbs of state,
Partners in honour, so ordained by fate;
Nearer in show, yet further off in love,
In which, the lowest always are above.
But whither am I carried in conceit?
My wit too weak to construe of the great.
Why not? Although we are but born of earth,
We may behold the heavens, despising death,
And loving Heaven that is so far above,
May in the end vouchsafe us entire love.
Therefore sweet memory do thou retain
Those pleasures past, which will not turn again;
Remember beauteous Dorset's former sports,
So far from being touched by ill reports,
Wherein my self did always bear a part
While reverend love presented my true heart.
Those recreations let me bear in mind,
Which her sweet youth and noble thoughts did find,
Whereof deprived, I evermore must grieve,
Hating blind fortune, careless to relieve.
And you, sweet Cookham, whom these ladies leave,
I now must tell the grief you did conceive
At their departure; when they went away,

How every thing retained a sad dismay.
Nay, long before, when once an inkling came,
Methought each thing did unto sorrow frame:
The trees that were so glorious in our view,
Forsook both flowers and fruit; when once they knew
Of your depart, their very leaves did wither,
Changing their colours as they grew together.
But when they saw they had no power to stay you,
They often wept, though, speechless, could not pray you,
Letting their tears in your fair bosoms fall,
As if they said, Why will ye leave us all?
This being vain, they cast their leaves away,
Hoping that pity would have made you stay:
Yet did I see a noble grateful mind,
Requiting each according to their kind;
Forgetting not to turn and take your leave
Of these sad creatures, powerless to receive
Your favour, when with grief you did depart,
Placing the former pleasures in your heart,
Giving great charge to noble memory,
There to preserve their love continually;
But specially the love of that fair tree,
That first and last you did vouchsafe to see,
In which it pleased you oft to take the air,
With noble Dorset, then a virgin fair,
Where many a learned book was read and scanned,
To this fair tree, taking me by the hand,
You did repeat the pleasures which had past,
Seeming to grieve they could no longer last,
And with a chaste, yet loving kiss took leave,
Of which sweet kiss I did it soon bereave,
Scorning a senseless creature should possess
So rare a favour, so great happiness.

No other kiss it could receive from me,
For fear to give it back what they took of thee:
So I ungrateful creature did deceive it,
Of that which you vouchsafed in love to leave it.
And though it oft had given me much content,
Yet this great wrong I never could repent:
But of the happiest made it most forlorn,
To show that nothing's free from fortunes scorn,
While all the rest with this most beauteous tree,
Made their sad consort sorrow's harmony.
The flowers that on the banks and walks did grow,
Crept in the ground, the grass did weep for woe.
The winds and waters seemed to chide together,
Because you went away they knew not whither,
And those sweet brooks that ran so fair and clear,
With grief and trouble wrinkled did appear.
Those pretty birds that wonted were to sing,
Now neither sing, nor chirp, nor use their wing,
But, with their tender feet on some bare spray,
Warble forth sorrow, and their own dismay.
Fair Philomela leaves her mournful ditty,
Drowned in dead sleep, yet can procure no pity.
Each arbour, bank, each seat, each stately tree,
Looks bare and desolate now for want of thee,
Turning green tresses into frosty grey,
While in cold grief they wither all away.
The sun grew weak, his beams no comfort gave,
While all green things did make the earth their grave:
Each briar, each bramble, when you went away,
Caught fast your clothes, thinking to make you stay:
Delightful Echo wanted to reply
To our last words, did now for sorrow die:
The house cast off each garment that might grace it,

Putting on dust and cobwebs to deface it.
All desolation then there did appear,
When you were going whom they held so dear.
This last farewell to Cookham here I give,
When I am dead thy name in this may live,
Wherein I have performed her noble hest,
Whose virtues lodge in my unworthy breast,
And ever shall, so long as life remains,
Tying my heart to her by those rich chains.

(1609–10)

Song

Love a child is ever crying;
    Please him, and he straight is flying;
    Give him he the more is craving,
    Never satisfied with having.

His desires have no measure;
    Endless folly is his treasure;
    What he promiseth he breaketh.
    Trust not one word that he speaketh.

He vows nothing but false matter,
    And to cozen you he'll flatter.
    Let him gain the hand, he'll leave you,
    And still glory to deceive you.

He will triumph in your wailing,
    And yet cause be of your failing.
    These his virtues are, and slighter
    Are his gifts, his favours lighter.

Feathers are as firm in staying,
    Wolves no fiercer in their preying.
    As a child then leave him crying,
    Nor seek him so given to flying.

(c.1610)

Chorus from *The Tragedy of Mariam*

'Tis not enough for one that is a wife
    To keep her spotless from an act of ill,
But from suspicion she should free her life,
    And bare herself of power as well as will.
'Tis not so glorious for her to be free,
As by her proper self restrained to be.

When she hath spacious ground to walk upon,
    Why on the ridge should she desire to go?
It is no glory to forbear alone
    Those things that may her honour overthrow,
But 'tis thankworthy, if she will not take
All lawful liberties for honour's sake.

The wife her hand against her fame doth rear,
    That more than to her lord alone will give
A private word to any second ear,
    And though she may with reputation live,
Yet though most chaste she doth her glory blot,
And wounds her honour, though she kills it not.

When to their husbands they themselves do bind,
    Do they not wholly give themselves away?
Or give they but their body, not their mind,
    Reserving that, though best, for others' prey?
No, sure, their thought no more can be their own,
And therefore should to none but one be known.

Then she usurps upon another's right,
    That seeks to be by public language graced,
And though her thoughts reflect with purest light

Her mind, if not peculiar, is not chaste.
For in a wife it is no worse to find
A common body, than a common mind.

(printed 1613)

To William Drummond of Hawthornden

I never rested on the Muses' bed,
Nor dipped my quill in the Thessalian fountain.
My rustic Muse was rudely fosteréd,
And flies too low to reach the double mountain.

Then do not sparks with your bright sun compare;
Perfection in a woman's work is rare.
From an untroubled mind should verses flow;
My discontents make mine too muddy show,
And hoarse encumbrances of household care.
Where these remain, the Muses ne'er repair.

If thou dost extol her hair,
Or her ivory forehead fair,
Or those stars, whose bright reflection
Thralls my heart in sweet subjection,
Or when to display thou seekest
The snow-mixed roses in her cheeks,
Or those rubies soft and sweet
Over those pretty rows that meet,
The Chian painter as ashamed
Hides his picture so far famed,
And the queen he carved it by
With a blush her face doth dye,
Since those lines do limn a creature
That so far surpassed her feature.
When thou showest how fair Flora
Pranked with pride the banks of Ora,
So thy verse her streams doth honour,
Strangers grow enamoured on her.

[21]

All the swans that swim in Po
Would their native brooks forgo,
And, as loathing Phœbus' beams,
Long to bathe in cooler streams.
Tree-turned Daphne would be seen
In her groves to flourish green,
And her boughs would gladly spare
To frame a garland for thy hair,
    That fairest nymphs with finest fingers
    May thee crown the best of singers.

But when thy Muse, dissolved in showers,
Wails that peerless prince of ours
Cropped by too untimely fate,
Her mourning doth exasperate
Senseless things. To see thee moan
Stones do weep and trees do groan;
Birds in air, fishes in flood,
Beasts in field forsake their food.
The nymphs forgoing all their bowers
Tear their chaplets decked with flowers.
Sol himself with misty vapour
Hides from earth his glorious taper,
    And as moved to hear thee plain
    Shows his grief in showers of rain.

*(c.*1616)

A Muzzle for Melastomus

If reason had but curbed thy witless will,
Or fear of God restrained thy raving quill,
Such venom foul thou wouldst have blushed to spew,
Except that grace have bidden thee adieu.
Prowess disdains to wrestle with the weak;
Heathenish-affected care not what they speak.

Seducer of the vulgar sort of men,
Was Satan crept into thy filthy pen,
Enflaming thee with such infernal smoke
That, if thou hadst will, should women choke?
Nefarious fiends thy sense herein deluded,
And from thee all humanity excluded.
Monster of men, worthy of no other name,
 For that thou didst essay our sex to shame.

(printed 1617)

When I first was brought to light,
(Rather into darkness thrown)
Midst of such a stormy night,
As in the dark could not be known
But unseen have passed untold,
Not among the rest enrolled,

Not a beam of light was seen;
Not a star peeped through the skies.
Fled from heaven the night's pale queen,
Nor my birth would patronise.
Blue the trembling tapers burned.
All fair eyes my blackness mourned.

The first light to greet mine eyes
Was the blaze of lightning flashes,
Which a proud tower raised to skies
In an instant struck to ashes.
In such darkness have I seen,
By such light still blinded been.

Me my sad forsaken mother
(Then her love eclipsed remaining)
Bred me not at first from other,
After from her breast sustaining
Me, who from her woes did borrow
But the pure extract of sorrow.

I was still brought up in woe.
Music pleased me not so well,
As of those that felt the blow

Weeping for to hear them tell
Of that storm, which threatening all
Only on our house did fall.

Other stories oft supplied,
Though our own might well content,
Being born on either side
To much woe by due descent.
And I would our race's fate
In my harms might terminate.

Mourning black best pleased mine eyes,
And methought became me best.
Sad and direful tragedies
Still I liked above the rest,
And those best I ever loved
Who most spite of fortune proved.

Saddest looks had sweetest grace,
Grieved with grief content yet showing.
Nought so well became the face,
As the cheeks with tears o'erflowing.
Wreathéd arms, neglected hair,
Best methought adorned the fair.

From my waking hour of birth
To this present weeping hour,
Never had I joy on earth,
But what served to make me more
Feel my harms, and brought with it
Greater ills, than that could quit.

My desires were ne'er effected
But where I mine ill desired;
Else they came so long protracted,

That the tide was back retired,
When they came and let me see
'Such as these thy wishes be'.

Any gift had fortune lent me
(Not that I can boast of many),
Any grace had nature sent me
(Yet I say I had not any),
Not so little can be thought
As were great the harms they brought.

Yet would mine accurséd star
Had in me his beams confined,
Whose infection spreading far
Struck at those to me were joined
In acquaintance, love and blood,
More or less as near they stood.

Some in their estates were wrecked,
Some proved luckless in their love,
Some with false defame were blacked,
Some their friends unkindness prove.
Those the least of ills have tried,
Who, alas, untimely died.

Thou most causeless wert forsaken
For a ruin-bringing love;
Death from thee thy love hath taken,
Left alone sad fates to prove.
Thee thy parents' fatal doom
Buries in a living tomb.

Happy thou hadst thy desire,
But your nuptial tapers set
Both your houses on a fire,

So from Troy the flame was fet.
Thou long-sought thy love didst find,
Find, alas, but proved unkind.

But thy woes should I awake,
Woes with thee in silence sleeping,
All the rest would theirs forsake,
Thine alone thought worth the weeping.
Had not fate cut off thy story,
Thine had robbed from mine the glory.

Yet for many harms of theirs,
And the greatest of mine own
Upon any of the spheres
Would I might the blame have thrown,
Whilst they of the ills they sent
Made myself the instrument.

Setting at the race's end
As the doubtful combat still,
Wheresoe'er my wishes bend,
As still tend to one they will,
There the loss still lights and brought
Farther mischiefs with it oft.

Help to any gave I ever,
Or advice to any lent,
Well to any wished I never
Where it came to good event.
But Oh! where most good of all
I desired, most ill did fall.

Thou whose harms were doubly mine,
Where least ill to have redeemed
Willingly I would resign

What my greatest good I deemed,
Not alone must wretched be,
But must owe the cause to me.

Whilst I gave myself for thee,
Of that gain yet may I boast,
And whilst thou to purchase me
All thy world besides hast cost.
By this match what have we won,
Both undoing and undone?

Not that I my woes desire,
Vented thus to make them less,
Or else pity thus require,
So to sweeten my distress.
Those which that had best deserved
Still are in my heart reserved.

But I set my griefs to show
Where nor light nor eyes are near,
And I story out my woe
Where there are no ears to hear,
But with silent words unfold
What by me shall ne'er be told.

*(c.*1620)

[28]

An Answer to my Lady Alice Egerton's Song

I cannot send you back my heart
    For I have but my own,
And as that sentry stands apart
    So watchman is alone.

Now I do leave you for to spy
    Where I my camp will place,
And if your scouts do bring allay
    Maybe yourself will face,

Then if you challenge me the field
    And would me battle set,
I then as master of the fields
    Perhaps may prove your net.

    *(c.*1644)

'ELIZA'

To my Husband

When from the world, I shall be ta'en,
And from earth's necessary pain,
Then let no blacks be worn for me,
Not in a ring, my dear, by thee,
But this bright diamond, let it be
Worn in remembrance of me,
And when it sparkles in your eye,
Think 'tis my shadow passeth by.
For why? More bright you shall me see
Than that or any gem can be.
Dress not the house with sable weed,
As if there were some dismal deed
Acted to be when I am gone.
There is no cause for me to mourn.
And let no badge of herald be
The sign of my antiquity.
It was my glory I did spring
From Heaven's eternal powerful King;
To His bright palace heir am I.
It is His promise. He'll not lie.
By my dear brother pray lay me.
It was a promise made by thee,
And now I must bid thee adieu,
For I'm a parting now from you.

(printed 1652)

A retired friendship, to Ardelia. 23 August 1651

Come, my Ardelia, to this bower
    Where, kindly mingling souls awhile,
Let's innocently spend an hour
    And at all serious follies smile.

Here is no quarrelling for crowns,
    Nor fear of changes in our fate,
No trembling at the great ones' frowns,
    Nor any slavery of state.

Here's no disguise, nor treachery,
    Nor any deep concealed design;
From blood and plots this place is free,
    And calm as are those looks of thine.

Here let us sit, and bless our stars
    Who did such happy quiet give,
As that removed from noise of wars
    In one another's hearts we live.

Why should we entertain a fear?
    Love cares not how the world is turned:
If crowds of dangers should appear,
    Yet friendship can be unconcerned.

We wear about us such a charm,
    No horror can be our offence,
For mischief's self can do no harm
    To friendship and to innocence.

Let's mark how soon Apollo's beams
    Command the flocks to quit their meat,

And not entreat the neighbour streams
    To quench their thirst, but cool their heat.

In such a scorching age as this,
    Whoever would not seek a shade
Deserve their happiness to miss,
    As having their own peace betrayed.

But we, of one another's mind
    Assured, the boisterous world disdain,
With quiet souls, and unconfined,
    Enjoy what princes wish in vain.

    (1651)

The Author to Her Book

Thou ill-formed offspring of my feeble brain,
Who after birth didst by my side remain,
Till snatched from thence by friends, less wise than true,
Who thee abroad, exposed to public view,
Made thee in rags, halting to the press to trudge,
Where errors were not lessened (all may judge).
At thy return my blushing was not small,
My rambling brat in print should mother call.
I cast thee by as one unfit for light,
Thy visage was so irksome in my sight.
Yet being mine own, at length affection would
Thy blemishes amend, if so I could.
I washed thy face, but more defects I saw,
And rubbing off a spot still made a flaw.
I stretched thy joints to make thee even feet,
Yet still thou run'st more hobbling than is meet.
In better dress to trim thee was my mind,
But nought save homespun cloth in the house I find.
In this array 'mongst vulgars may'st thou roam;
In critic's hands beware thou dost not come,
And take thy way where yet thou art not known.
If for thy father asked, say thou hadst none,
And for thy mother, she alas is poor,
Which caused her thus to send thee out of door.

(after 1650, before 1672)

The Hunting of the Hare

Betwixt two ridges of ploughed-land, lay Wat,
Pressing his body close to earth lay squat.
His nose upon his two fore-feet close lies,
Glaring obliquely with his great grey eyes.
His head he always sets against the wind;
If turn his tail, his hairs blow up behind,
Then he too cold will grow, but he is wise,
And keeps his coat still down, so warm he lies.
Thus resting all the day, till sun doth set,
Then riseth up, his relief for to get,
Walking about until the sun doth rise,
Then back returns, down in his form he lies.
At last, poor Wat was found, as he there lay,
By huntsmen, with their dogs which came that way.
Seeing, gets up and fast begins to run,
Hoping some ways the cruel dogs to shun,
But they by nature have so quick a scent,
That by their nose they trace what way he went,
And with their deep, wide mouths set forth a cry,
Which answered was by echoes in the sky.
Then Wat was struck with terror, and with fear,
Thinks every shadow still the dogs they were,
And running out some distance from the noise
To hide himself, his thoughts he new employs.
Under a clod of earth in sand-pit wide,
Poor Wat sat close, hoping himself to hide.
There long he had not sat, but straight his ears
The winding horns and crying dogs he hears.
Starting with fear, up leaps, then doth he run,

And with such speed, the ground scarce treads upon.
Into a great thick wood he straightway gets,
Where underneath a broken bough he sits.
At every leaf that with the wind did shake,
Did bring such terror, made his heart to ache.
That place he left, to champain plains he went,
Winding about, for to deceive their scent,
And while they snuffling were, to find his track,
Poor Wat, being weary, his swift place did slack.
On his two hinder legs for ease did sit,
His fore-feet rubbed his face from dust and sweat.
Licking his feet, he wiped his ears so clean,
That none could tell that Wat had hunted been,
But, casting round about his fair great eyes,
The hounds in full career he near him spies.
To Wat it was so terrible a sight,
Fear gave him wings, and made his body light.
Though weary was before, by running long,
Yet now his breath he never felt more strong.
Like those that dying are, think health returns,
When 'tis but a faint blast, which life out burns,
For spirits seek to guard the heart about,
Striving with Death, but Death doth quench them out.
Thus they so fast came on, with such loud cries,
That he no hopes hath left, nor help espies.
With that the winds did pity poor Wat's case,
And with their breath the scent blew from the place.
Then every nose is busily employed,
And every nostril is set open wide,
And every head doth seek a several way,
To find what grass, or track, the scent on lay.
Thus quick industry, that is not slack,
Is like to witchery, brings lost things back,

For though the wind had tied the scent up close,
A busy dog thrust in his snuffling nose,
And drew it out, with it did foremost run,
Then horns blew loud, for the rest to follow on.
The great slow hounds, their throats did set a base,
The fleet swift hounds as tenors next in place,
The little beagles they a treble sing,
And through the air their voice around did ring,
Which made a consort, as they ran along,
If they but words could speak, might sing a song.
The horns kept time, the hunters shout for joy,
And valiant seem, poor Wat for to destroy:
Spurring their horses to a full career,
Swim rivers deep, leap ditches without fear,
Endanger life, and limbs, so fast will ride,
Only to see how patiently Wat died.
For why, the dogs so near his heels did get,
That they their sharp teeth in his breech did set.
Then tumbling down, did fall with weeping eyes,
Gives up his ghost, and thus poor Wat he dies.
Men whooping loud such acclamations make,
As if the Devil they did prisoner take,
When they do but a shiftless Creature kill.
To hunt, there needs no valiant soldier's skill,
But Man doth think that exercise and toil
To keep their health, is best which makes most spoil,
Thinking that food, and nourishments so good,
And appetite that feeds on flesh, and blood.
When they do lions, wolves, bears, tigers see,
To kill poor sheep, straight say, they cruel be,
But for themselves all creatures think too few,
For luxury, wish God would make them new,
As if that God made creatures for Man's meat,

To give them life and sense for man to eat,
Or else for sport, for recreation's sake
Destroy those lives that God saw good to make,
Making their stomachs graves, which full they fill
With murdered bodies, that in sport they kill.
Yet Man doth think himself so gentle, mild,
When he of creatures is most cruel wild.
And is so proud, thinks only he shall live,
That God a god-like nature did him give,
And that all creatures for his sake alone,
Were made for him to tyrannise upon.

(printed 1653)

A Song to excite spiritual Joy

The Winter being over,
In order comes the Spring,
Which doth green herbs discover,
And cause the birds to sing.
The night also expirèd,
Then comes the morning bright,
Which is so much desirèd
By all that love the light.
This may learn
Them that mourn,
To put their grief to flight:
The Spring succeedeth Winter,
And day must follow night.

He therefore that sustaineth
Affliction or distress,
Which every member paineth,
And findeth no release:
Let such therefore despair not,
And therefore must have end.
They that faint
With complaint
Therefore are to blame:
They add to their afflictions,
And amplify the same.

For if they could with patience
A while possess the mind,
By inward consolations
They might refreshing find,

To sweeten all their crosses
That little time they endure,
So might they gain by losses,
And sharp would sweet procure;
But if the mind
Be inclined
To unquietness,
That only may be called
The worst of all distress.

He that is melancholy,
Detesting all delight,
His wits by sottish folly
Are ruinated quite.
Sad discontent and murmurs
To him are incident;
Were he possessed of honours,
He would not be content.
Sparks of joy
Fly away.
Floods of cares arise,
And all delightful motion
In the conception dies.

But those that are contented,
However things do fall,
Much anguish is prevented,
And they soon freed from all.
They finish all their labours
With much felicity.
Their joy in troubles savours
Of perfect piety.
Cheerfulness
Doth express

A settled pious mind,
Which is not prone to grudging,
From murmuring refined.

Lascivious joy I praise not,
Neither do it allow,
For when the same decays not,
No branch of peace can grow.
For why, it is as sinister
As is excessive grief,
And does the heart sequester
From all good. To be brief
Vain delight
Passeth quite
The bounds of modesty,
And makes one apt to nothing
But sensuality.

(printed 1653)

On My Boy Henry

Here lies a boy, the finest child from me,
Which makes my heart and soul sigh for to see,
Nor can I think of any thought, but grieve,
For joy or pleasure could me not relieve;
It lived days as many as my years,
No more, which caused my grievéd tears;
Twenty and nine was the number,
And death hath parted us asunder;
But you are happy, sweetest, on high,
I mourn not for thy birth, nor cry.

(1656)

Upon the sight of my abortive birth
the 31st of December 1657

What birth is this, a poor despiséd creature?
    A little embryo, void of life, and feature.

Seven times I went my time, when mercy giving
    deliverance unto me and mine, all living,

Strong, right proportioned, lovely girls and boys,
    Their father's, mother's present, hoped-for joys.

That was great wisdom, goodness, power, love, praise
    to my dear Lord, lovely in all his ways.

This is no less. The same God hath it done.
    Submits my heart: that's better than a son.

In giving, taking, stroking, striking, still
    His glory and my good is His my will

In that then, this now, both, good God most mild.
    His will's more dear to me than any child.

I also joy, that God hath gained one more
    To praise him in the heavens than was before,

And that this babe, as well as all the rest,
    since it had a soul, shall be for ever blest.

That I'm made instrumental to both these –
    God's praise, babes' bliss – it highly doth me please.

Maybe the Lord looks for more thankfulness
    and high esteem for those I do possess.

As limners draw dead shades for to set forth
    their lively colours and their pictures' worth,

So doth my God, in this as all things wise,
    By my dead formless babe teach me to prize

My living pretty pair, Nat and Bethia,
    the children dear God yet lends to Maria.

Praised be His name. This two's full compensation
    For all that's gone and that in expectation,

And if herein God hath fulfilled His will,
    His hand-maid's pleased, completely happy still.

I only now desire of my sweet God
    the reason why He took in hand His rod.

What He doth spy? what is the thing amiss?
    I fain would learn, whilst I the rod do kiss.

Methinks I hear God's voice: 'This is thy sin,'
    (And conscience justifies the same within)

'Thou often dost present me with dead fruit.
    Why should not my returns, thy presents suit?

'Dead duties, prayers, praises, thou dost bring,
    affections dead, dead heart in everything,

'In hearing, reading, conference, meditation,
    in acting, graces and in conversation.

'Who's taught or bettered by you? No relation.
    Thou art cause of mourning, not of imitation.

'Thou dost not answer that great means I give.
    My word, and ordinances do teach to live.

'Lively, oh, do it'. Thy mercies are most sweet,
    Chastisements sharp and all the means that's meet.

'Mend now my child, and lively fruit bring me,
    so thou advantaged much by this wilt be.'

My dearest Lord, Thy charge and more is true.
    I see it, am humbled, and for pardon sue.

In Christ forgive and henceforth I will be –
    'What?' Nothing, Lord; but what Thou makest me.

I am nought, have nought, can do nothing but sin,
    as my experience saith, for I've been in

Several conditions, trials great and many.
    In all I find my nothingness; not any-

Thing do I own but sin. Christ is my all,
    that I do want, can crave; or ever shall.

That good that suiteth all my whole desires
    and for me unto God, all he requires,

It is in Christ. He's mine, and I am His.
    This union is my only happiness;

But, Lord, since I'm a child by mercy free,
    Let me by filial fruits much honour Thee.

I'm a branch of the vine. Purge me therefore,
    Father, more fruit to bring than heretofore.

A plant in God's house, Oh! that I may be,
    more flourishing in age, a growing tree.

Let not my heart, as doth my womb, miscarry,
    but, precious means received, let it tarry

Till it be formed of gospel's shape and suit,
    my means, my mercies, and be pleasant fruit.

In my whole life, lively do thou make me.
    For Thy praise and name's sake, Oh, quicken me!

Lord, I beg quickening grace. That grace afford!
    Quicken me, Lord, according to Thy Word.

It is a lovely boon I make to Thee.
    After Thy loving kindness, quicken me.

Thy quickening spirit unto me convey;
    and thereby quicken me, in Thine own way.

And let the presence of Thy spirit dear
    be witnessed by His fruits. Let them appear

To, for Thee: love, joy, peace, gentleness,
    long-suffering, goodness, faith and much meekness.

And let my walking in the Spirit say,
    I live in it and desire it to obey,

And since my heart Thou'st lifted up to Thee,
    amend it, Lord and keep it still with Thee.

Saith Maria Carey
always in Christ happy.

January 12, 1657

Verses

All sorts of men through various labours press
To the same end, contented quietness;
Great princes vex their labouring thoughts to be
Possessed of an unbounded sovereignty;
The hardy soldier doth all his toils sustain
That he may conquer first, and after reign;
Th'industrious merchant ploughs the angry seas
That he may bring home wealth, and live at ease.
These none of them attain, for sweet repose
But seldom to the splendid palace goes.
A troop of restless passions wander there,
And private lives are only free from care.
Sleep to the cottage bringeth happy nights,
But to the court hung round with flaring lights,
Which th'office of the vanished day supply,
His image only comes to close the eye,
But gives the troubled mind no ease of care,
While country slumbers undisturbéd are,
Where, if the active fancy dreams present
They bring no horrors to the innocent.
Ambition doth incessantly aspire,
And each advance leads on to new desire,
Nor yet can riches av'rice satisfy,
For want and wealth together multiply,
Nor can voluptuous men more fullness find,
For enjoyed pleasures leave their stings behind.
He's only rich who knows no want; he reigns
Whose will no severe tyranny constrains;

And he alone possesseth true delight
Whose spotless soul no guilty fears affright.
This freedom in the country life is found,
Where innocence and safe delights abound.
Here man's a prince; his subjects ne'er repine
When on his back their wealthy fleeces shine.
If for his appetite the fattest die,
Those who survive will raise no mutiny.
His table is with home-got dainties crowned,
With friends, not flatterers, encompassed round.
No spies nor traitors on his trencher wait,
Nor is his mirth confined to rules of state.
An arméd guard he neither hath nor needs,
Nor fears a poisoned morsel when he feeds.
Bright constellations hang above his head;
Beneath his feet are flow'ry carpets spread.
The merry birds delight him with their songs,
And healthful air his happy life prolongs.
At harvest merrily his flocks he shears,
And in cold weather their warm fleeces wears.
Unto his ease he fashions all his clothes;
His cup with uninfected liquor flows.
The vulgar breath doth not his thoughts elate,
Nor can he be o'erwhelméd by their hate.
Yet, if ambitiously he seeks for fame,
One village feast shall gain a greater name
Than his who wears the imperial diadem,
Whom the rude multitude do still condemn.
Sweet peace and joy his blest companions are;
Fear, sorrow, envy, lust, revenge and care,
And all that troop which breeds the world's offence,
With pomp and majesty, are banish'd thence.

What court then can such liberty afford?
Or where is man so uncontrolled a lord?

(1658)

APHRA BEHN

In Imitation of Horace

What mean those amorous curls of jet?
    For what heart-ravished maid
Dost thou thy hair in order set?
    Thy wanton tresses braid?
And thy vast store of beauties open lay,
That the deluded fancy leads astray?

For pity hide thy starry eyes,
    Whose languishments destroy,
And look not on the slave that dies
    With an excess of joy.
Defend thy coral lips, thy amber breath;
To taste these sweets lets in a certain death.

Forbear, fond charming youth, forbear
    Thy words of melting love;
Thy eyes thy language well may spare,
    One dart enough can move,
And she that hears thy voice and sees thy eyes
With too much pleasure, too much softness dies.

Cease, cease with sighs to warm my soul,
    Or press me with thy hand.
Who can the kindling fire control,
    The tender force withstand?
Thy sighs and touches like wingéd lightning fly,
And are the gods of Love's artillery.

(printed 1684)

Song

Strephon has fashion, wit and youth,
    With all things else that please.
He nothing wants but love and truth
    To ruin me with ease.

But he is flint, and bears the art
    To kindle strong desire.
His power inflames another heart.
    Yet he ne'er feels the fire.

Alas, it does my soul perplex,
    When I his charms recall,
To think he should despise the sex,
Or, what's worse, love them all.

My weary heart, like Noah's dove
    That seeks in vain for rest,
Finding no hope to fix my love,
    Returns into my breast.

(printed 1684)

to J.G.

Tell me you hate, and flatter me no more.
By Heaven I do not wish you should adore.
With humbler blessings I content can be;
I only beg that you would pity me
In as much silence as I first designed
To bear the raging torture of my mind,
For when your eyes first made my heart your slave
I thought to have hid my fetters in my grave.
Heaven witness for me that I strove to hide
My violent love, and my fond eyes did chide
For glancing at thee, and my blushes hid,
With as much care as ever virgin did,
And though I languished with the greatest pain
That e'er despairing lover did sustain,
I ne'er in public did let fall a tear,
Nor breathed a sigh in reach of any ear.
Yet I in private drew no breath but sighs,
And showers of tears fell from my wretched eyes.
The lilies left my front, the rose my cheeks;
My nights were spent in sobs and sudden shrieks.
I felt my strength insensibly decayed
And Death approach, but ah! then you conveyed
Soft amorous tales unto my listening ears,
And gentle vows and well-becoming tears,
Then deeper oaths, nor e'er your siege removed
Till I confessed my flame, and owned I loved.
Your kinder smiles had raised my flames so high
That all at distance might the fire descry.
I took no care my passion to suppress

Nor hide the love I thought I did possess,
But, ah! too late I find your love was such
As gallants pay in course, or scarce so much.
You shun my sight; you feed me with delays;
You slight, affront; a thousand several ways
You do torment with studied cruelty,
And yet alternately you flatter me.
Oh! if you love not, plainly say you hate,
And give my miseries a shorter date –
'Tis kinder than to linger out my fate.
And yet I could with less regret have died
A victim to your coldness than your pride.

(printed 1679)

An Epistle

Is friendship fled, or love grown cold?
Do frozen walls of ice withhold
Its pearly streams? O let the sun,
That gave it being, shine upon
The brittle fence! or is some screen
Injuriously set up between
The gentle spring, and that bright ray
Which, conquering night, brings joyful day?
Remove that obstacle away.
Then, though with grief I may confess
In wintertime the effects be less,
Because of distance or cold air
Prevailing in our hemisphere,
And interposing (for Sol's power
Is still the same each day and hour).
It will dissolve the frost in time,
If its warm ray thereon may shine.
Though vacant clouds do interpose
Its pure refulgent beam, and those
Inferior concretes that have birth
From the gross element of earth.
But stay! Methinks a spring should be
From winter's chilling force more free
Than to be frozen! Inbred heat
Is then, with purest springs, more great,
And with its current soon doth glide
Through ice besetting either side.

Let love spring up, that we may see
The same effects, dear friend, in thee.

   (1682)

My Fate

Raising my drooping head, o'ercharged with thought,
Having each scene of life before me brought,
I chide my self because I durst repine
At nature's laws, or those that were divine.
Throughout the whole creation 'tis the same,
The fuel is devoured by the flame.
Each peaceful, harmless, unoffending thing
Is to the offender made an offering,
Even God Himself. – Hold, my aspiring thought!
Descend, my Muse, thy flight too high is wrought.
Tell not how He, all peaceful, and all kind,
Was offered for the vilest of mankind,
A victim for the vilest was designed.
Descend, I say, my Muse! Low things afford
Themes high enough for thee. Touch not the Word
Till He hath touched thy wings with grace divine,
Then, only His, thou shalt the world decline. –
The harmless dove the falcon doth betray,
The lamb is to the wolf become a prey,
And man, to whom free will Heaven doth impart
To follow still the counsels of his heart,
Is racked with doubt. If harmless, he designs
Peace to his heart, and still his wish confines,
Justice to peace, and love to quiet joins.
Why then, the dove-like fate will sure be his:
Short is his life, unsettled is his bliss.
Hard fate; that choice we eagerly pursue,
Is, or to be undone, or to undo.

(before 1685)

ELIZABETH SINGER, later ROWE ('PHILOMELA')

To a very young Gentleman at a Dancing-School

So when the Queen of Love rose from the seas,
Divinely fair in such a blest amaze,
The enamoured watery deities did gaze,

As we when charming Flammin did surprize,
More heavenly bright, our whole seraglio's eyes,
And not a nymph her wonder could disguise,

Whilst with a lovely pride the graceful boy
Passed all the ladies, like a sultan, by,
Only he looked more absolute and coy.

When with a haughty air he did advance
To lead out some transported she to dance,
He gave his hand as carelessly as chance,

Attended with a universal sigh.
On her each beauty cast a jealous eye
And quite fell out with guiltless destiny.

(1692)

Upon the Saying that My Verses were made by Another

Next Heaven, my vows to thee, Oh sacred Muse!
I offered up, nor didst thou them refuse.

'Oh queen of verse,' said I, 'if thou'lt inspire,
And warm my soul with thy poetic fire,
No love of gold shall share with thee my heart,
Or yet ambition in my breast have part.
More rich, more noble I will ever hold
The Muse's laurel than a crown of gold.
An undivided sacrifice I'll lay
Upon thine altar, soul and body pay.
Thou shalt my pleasure, my employment be;
My all I'll make a holocaust to thee.'

The deity that ever does attend
Prayers so sincere to mine did condescend.
I writ, and the judicious praised my pen.
Could any doubt ensuing glory then?
What pleasing raptures filled my ravished sense!
How strong, how sweet, Fame, was thy influence!
And thine, false hope, that to my flattered sight
Didst glories represent so near and bright!
By thee deceived, methought each verdant tree
Apollo's transformed Daphne seemed to be;
And every fresher branch, and every bough
Appeared as garlands to empale my brow.
The learned in love say, thus the wingéd boy
Does first approach, dressed up in welcome joy;
At first he to the cheated lover's sight

Nought represents but rapture and delight,
Alluring hopes, soft fears, which stronger bind
Their hearts, than when they more assurance find.

　　Emboldened thus, to fame I did commit,
By some few hands, my most unlucky wit.
But ah, the sad effects that from it came!
What ought to have bought me honour, bought me
　　shame!
Like Æsop's painted jay, I seemed to all,
Adorned in plumes, I not my own could call:
Rifled like her, each one my feathers tore,
And, as they thought, unto their owner bore.
My laurels thus another's brow adorned,
My numbers they admired but me they scorned:
Another's brow that had so rich a store
Of sacred wreaths that circled it before,
Where mine, quite lost, like a small stream that ran
Into a vast, and boundless ocean,
Was swallowed up with what it joined, and drowned,
And that abyss yet no accession found.

　　Orinda, Albion's and her sex's grace,
Owed not her glory to her beauteous face.
It was her radiant soul that shone within,
Which struck a lustre through her outward skin,
That did her lips and cheeks with roses dye,
Advanced her height and sparkled in her eye.
Nor did her sex obstruct her fame,
But higher 'mong the stars it fixed her name;
What she did write, not only all allowed,
But every laurel to her laurel bowed.

[58]

The envious age only to me alone
Will not allow what I do write my own,
But let them rage and 'gainst a maid conspire,
So deathless numbers from my tuneful lyre
Do ever flow. So, Phœbus, I by thee
Inspired divinely, and possessed may be,
I willingly accept Cassandra's fate,
To speak the truth, although believed too late.

(before 1685)

A Virgin Life

Since, gracious Heaven, you have bestowed on me
So great a kindness for virginity,
Suffer me not to fall into the power
Of Man's almost omnipotent amour,
But in this happy state let me remain,
And in chaste verse my chaster thoughts explain,
Fearless of twenty-five and all its rage,
When time and beauty endless wars engage,
And fearless of that antiquated name
Which oft makes happy maid turn hapless dame.
The scorns fixed to that name our sex betray,
And often make us fling ourselves away,
As harmless kids which when pursued by men
For safety run into a lion's den.
Ah lovely state! how strange it is to see
What mad conceptions some have made of thee!
As if thy being was all wretchedness,
Or foul deformity in the ugliest dress,
Whereas thy beauty's pure, celestial,
Thy thoughts divine, thy words angelical,
And such ought all thy votaries to be,
Or else they're so but for necessity.
A virgin bears the impress of all good;
Under that name, all virtue's understood.
So equal all, her looks, her mien, her dress,
That nought but modesty seems in excess.
When virgins any treats or visits make,
'Tis not for tattle but for friendship's sake.
The neighbouring poor are her adopted heirs,

And less she cares for her own good than theirs,
And by obedience testifies she can
Be as good a subject as the stoutest man.
She to her church such filial duty pays,
That one would think she lived in the pristine days.
Her whole life's business she drives to these ends,
To serve her God, her neighbour and her friends.

(printed 1688, revised c. 1701)

The Liberty

Shall I be one of those obsequious fools
That square their lives by Custom's scanty rules?
Condemned forever to the puny curse
Of precepts taught at boarding-school or nurse,
That all the business of my life must be
Foolish, dull, trifling formality?
Confined to a strict magic complaisance
And round a circle of nice visits dance,
Nor for my life beyond the chalk advance?
The devil Censure stands to guard the same;
One step awry, he tears my venturous fame,
So when my friends, in a facetious vein
With mirth and wit a while can entertain,
Though ne'er so pleasant, yet I must not stay,
If a commanding clock bids me away,
But with a sudden start, as in a fright,
'I must be gone indeed! 'Tis after eight!'
Sure these restraints with such regret we bear
That dreaded Censure can't be more severe,
Which has no terror if we did not fear,
But let the bugbear timorous infants fright.
I'll not be scared from innocent delight.
Whatever is not vicious I dare do.
I'll never to the idol Custom bow
Unless it suits with my own humour too.
Some boast their fetters of formality,
Fancy they ornamental bracelets be;
I'm sure they're gyves and manacles to me.
To their dull, fulsome rules I'll not be tied,

For all the flattery that exalts their pride.
My sex forbids I should my silence break;
I lose my jest, 'cause women must not speak.
Mysteries must not be with my search profaned;
My closet not with books but sweetmeats crammed,
A little china to advance the show,
My prayerbook and *Seven Champions* or so.
My pen, if ever used, employed must be
In lofty themes of useful housewifery,
Transcribing old receipts of cookery,
And what is necessary among the rest,
Good cures for agues and a cancered breast,
But I can't here write my *probatum est*.
My daring pen will bolder sallies make
And, like myself, an unchecked freedom take,
Not chained to the nice order of my sex,
And with restraints my wishing soul perplex.
I'll blush at sin, and not what some call shame,
Secure my virtue, slight precarious fame.
This courage speaks me brave. 'Tis surely worse
To keep those rules which privately we curse,
And I'll appeal to all the formal saints
With what reluctance they endure restraints.

(printed 1703)

To the Ladies

Wife and servant are the same,
But only differ in the name,
For when the fatal knot is tied,
Which nothing, nothing can divide,
When she the word *obey* has said,
And Man by law supreme has made,
Then all that's kind is laid aside,
And nothing left but state and pride.
Fierce as an eastern prince he grows,
And all his innate rigour shows.
Then but to look, to laugh, or speak
Will the nuptial contract break.
Like mutes she signs alone must make
And never any freedom take,
But still be governed by a nod
And fear her husband as her God,
Him still must serve, him still obey,
And nothing act, and nothing say,
But what her haughty Lord thinks fit,
Who with the power, has all the wit.
Then shun, oh! shun that wretched state,
And all the fawning flatterers hate.
Value your selves, and men despise.
You must be proud, if you'll be wise.

(Poems on Several Occasions, 1703)

Verses written on her Death-bed at Bath
to her Husband in London

Thou who dost all my worldly thoughts employ,
Thou pleasing source of all my earthly joy,
Thou tenderest husband and thou dearest friend,
To thee this first, this last adieu I send.
At length the conqueror Death asserts his right,
And will for ever veil me from thy sight.
He woos me to him with a cheerful grace,
And not one terror clouds his meagre face.
He promises a lasting rest from pain,
And shows that all life's fleeting joys are vain.
The eternal scenes of Heaven he sets in view,
And tells me that no other joys are true,
But love, fond love, would yet resist his power,
Would fain awhile defer the parting hour.
He brings thy mourning image to my eyes,
And would obstruct my journey to the skies.
But say, thou dearest, thou unwearied friend,
Say, shouldst thou grieve to see my sorrows end?
Thou knowest a painful pilgrimage I've passed,
And shouldst thou grieve that rest is come at last?
Rather rejoice to see me shake off life,
And die, as I have lived, thy faithful wife.

(1715)

The Forsaken Wife

Methinks 'tis strange you can't afford
One pitying look, one parting word.
Humanity claims this as its due,
But what's humanity to you?

Cruel man! I am not blind;
Your infidelity I find.
Your want of love my ruin shows,
My broken heart, your broken vows.
Yet maugre all your rigid hate
I will be true in spite of fate,
And one preëminence I'll claim,
To be forever still the same.

Show me a man that dare be true,
That dares to suffer what I do,
That can forever sigh unheard,
And ever love without regard,
I will then own your prior claim
To love, to honour and to fame,
But till that time, my dear, adieu.
I yet superior am to you.

(Miscellany Poems on Several Subjects, 1722)

A Nocturnal Reverie

In such a night, when every louder wind
Is to its distant cavern safe confined,
And only gentle Zephyr fans his wings,
And lonely Philomel, still waking, sings,
Or from some tree, famed for the owl's delight,
She, hollowing clear, directs the wanderer right,
In such a night, when passing clouds give place,
Or thinly veil the heavens' mysterious face,
When in some river, overhung with green,
The waving moon and trembling leaves are seen,
When freshened grass now bears itself upright,
And makes cool banks to pleasing rest invite,
Whence springs the woodbind, and the bramble-rose,
And where the sleepy cowslip sheltered grows,
Whilst now a paler hue the foxglove takes,
Yet checquers still with red the dusky brakes,
When scattered glow-worms, but in twilight fine,
Show trivial beauties watch their hour to shine,
(Whilst Salisbury stands the test of every light,
In perfect charms, and perfect virtue bright)
When odours, which declined repelling day
Through temperate air uninterrupted stray,
When darkened groves their softest shadows wear,
And falling waters we distinctly hear,
When through the gloom more venerable shows
Some ancient fabric, awful in repose,
While sunburnt hills their swarthy looks conceal,
And swelling haycocks thicken up the vale,
When the loosed horse now, as his pasture leads,

Comes slowly grazing through the adjoining meads,
Whose stealing pace, and lengthened shade we fear,
Till torn-up forage in his teeth we hear,
When nibbling sheep at large pursue their food,
And unmolested kine rechew the cud,
When curlews cry beneath the village-walls,
And to her straggling brood the partridge calls,
Their shortlived jubilee the creatures keep,
Which but endures, whilst tyrant-man does sleep,
When a sedate content the spirit feels,
And no fierce light disturbs, whilst it reveals,
But silent musings urge the mind to seek
Something, too high for syllables to speak.
Till the free soul to a composedness charmed,
Finding the elements of rage disarmed,
O'er all below a solemn quiet grown,
Joys in the inferior world, and thinks it like her own.
In such a night let me abroad remain,
Till morning breaks, and all's confused again,
Our cares, our toils, our clamours are renewed,
Or pleasure, seldom reached, again pursued.

(1711)

An Answer to a Love-Letter in Verse

Is it to me, this sad lamenting strain?
Are Heaven's choicest gifts bestowed in vain?
A plenteous fortune, and a beauteous bride,
Your love rewarded, and content your pride?
Yet leaving her, 'tis me that you pursue,
Without one single charm but being new.
    How vile is man! how I detest the ways
Of artful falsehood, and designing praise!
Tasteless, an easy happiness you slight,
Ruin your joy, and mischief your delight.
Why should poor pug, the mimic of your kind,
Wear a rough chain, and be to box confined?
Some cup, perhaps, he breaks, or tears a fan,
While moves unpunished the destroyer, Man.
Not bound by vows, and unrestrained by shame,
In sport you break the heart, and rend the fame.
Not that your art can be successful here,
The already plundered need no robber fear,
Nor sighs, nor charms, nor flattery can move,
Too well secured against a second love.
Once, and but once, that devil charmed my mind.
To reason deaf, to observation blind,
I idly hoped (what cannot love persuade?)
My fondness equalled, and my truth repaid.
Slow to distrust, and willing to believe,
Long hushed my doubts, and would myself deceive;
But oh! too soon – this tale would ever last –
Sleep, sleep my wrongs, and let me think them past.
    For you, who mourn with counterfeited grief,

And ask so boldly like a begging thief,
May soon some other nymph inflict the pain
You know so well with cruel art to feign.
Though long you've sported with Dan Cupid's dart,
You may see eyes, and you may feel a heart.
So the brisk wits, who stop the evening coach,
Laugh at the fear that follows their approach,
With idle mirth, and haughty scorn despise
The passenger's pale cheek and staring eyes,
But, seized by Justice, find a fright no jest,
And all the terror doubled in their breast.

(*c.*1720)

Wedlock. A Satire

Thou tyrant, whom I will not name,
Whom Heaven and Hell alike disclaim,
Abhorred and shunned, for different ends,
By angels, Jesuits, beasts and fiends,
What terms to curse thee shall I find,
Thou plague peculiar to mankind?
Oh may my verse excel in spite
The wiliest, wittiest imps of night!
Then lend me for a while your rage,
You maidens old and matrons sage,
So may my terms in railing seem
As vile and hateful as my theme.

Eternal foe to soft desires,
Inflamer of forbidden fires,
Thou source of discord, pain and care,
Thou sure forerunner of despair,
Thou scorpion with a double face,
Thou lawful plague of human race,
Thou bane of freedom, ease and mirth,
Thou deep damnation upon earth,
Thou serpent which the angels fly,
Thou monster whom the beasts defy,
Whom wily Jesuits sneer at too,
And Satan, let him have his due,
Was never so confirmed a dunce
To risk damnation more than once.
That wretch, if such a wretch there be,
Who hopes for happiness from thee,

May search successfully as well
For truth in whores and ease in Hell.

(c. 1730)

A Prayer for Indifference

Oft I've implored the gods in vain,
    And prayed till I've been weary;
Once more I'll try my wish to gain
    Of Oberon, the fairy.

Sweet airy being, wanton sprite,
    That liv'st in woods unseen,
And oft by Cynthia's silver light
    Tripst gaily o'er the green;

If e'er thy pitying heart was moved,
    As ancient stories tell,
And for the Athenian maid who loved,
    Thou soughtst a wondrous spell,

Oh, deign once more to exert thy power!
    Haply some herb or tree,
Sovereign as juice from western flower,
    Conceals a balm for me.

I ask no kind return in love,
    No tempting charm to please;
Far from the heart such gifts remove,
    That sighs for peace and ease.

Nor ease nor peace that heart can know,
    That, like the needle true,
Turns at the touch of joy or woe,
    But, turning, trembles too.

Far as distress the soul can wound.
    'Tis pain in each degree.

Bliss goes but to a certain bound;
   Beyond is agony.

Take then this treacherous sense of mine,
   Which dooms me still to smart,
Which pleasure can to pain refine,
   To pain new pangs impart.

Oh! haste to shed the sovereign balm.
   My shattered nerves new string,
And for my guest, serenely calm,
   The nymph Indifference bring.

At her approach, see Hope, see Fear,
   See Expectation fly,
With Disappointment in the rear,
   That blasts the promised joy.

The tears, which pity taught to flow,
   My eyes shall then disown;
The heart, that throbbed at others' woe,
   Shall then scarce feel its own.

The wounds, which now each moment bleed,
   Each moment then shall close,
And peaceful days shall still succeed
   To nights of sweet repose.

Oh, fairy elf, but grant me this,
   This one kind comfort send,
And so may never-fading bliss
   Thy flowery paths attend!

So may the glow-worm's glimmering light
   Thy tiny footsteps lead

To some new region of delight,
    Unknown to mortal tread;

And be thy acorn goblets filled
    With heaven's ambrosial dew,
From sweetest, freshest flowers distilled,
    That shed fresh sweets for you.

And what of life remains for me
    I'll pass in sober ease;
Half-pleased, contented will I be,
    Contented, half to please.

   (1758)

Sonnet. December Morning

I love to rise ere gleams the tardy light,
Winter's pale dawn; – and as warm fires illume,
And cheerful tapers shine around the room,
Through misty windows bend my musing sight
Where, round the dusky lawn, the mansions white,
With shutters closed, peer faintly through the gloom,
That slow recedes, while yon grey spires assume,
Rising from their dark pile, an added height
By indistinctness given. – Then to decree
The grateful thoughts to God, ere they unfold
To Friendship, or the Muse, or seek with glee
Wisdom's rich page! – O, hours! more worth than gold,
By whose blest use we lengthen life, and, free
From drear decays of age, outlive the old!

(19 December 1782)

This sonnet was written in an Apartment of the West Front of the Bishop's
Palace at Lichfield, inhabited by the Author from her thirteenth year. It looks
upon the Cathedral-Area, a green lawn encircled by Prebendal Houses, which
are white from being rough-cast.

Written near a port on a dark evening

Huge vapours brood above the clifted shore,
Night on the ocean settles, dark and mute,
Save where is heard the repercussive roar
Of drowsy billows, on the rugged foot
Of rocks remote; or still more distant tone
Of seamen in the anchored bark that tell
The watch relieved; or one deep voice alone
Singing the hour, and bidding 'Strike the bell.'
All is black shadow, but the lucid line
Marked by the light surf on the level sand,
Or where afar the ship-lights faintly shine
Like wandering fairy fires, that oft on land
Mislead the pilgrim – such the dubious ray
That wavering reason lends, in life's long darkling way.

(1784)

January, 1795

Pavement slippery, people sneezing,
Lords in ermine, beggars freezing;
Titled gluttons dainties carving,
Genius in a garret starving.

Lofty mansions, warm and spacious;
Courtiers cringing and voracious;
Misers scarce the wretched heeding;
Gallant soldiers fighting, bleeding.

Wives who laugh at passive spouses;
Theatres, and meeting-houses;
Balls, where simpering misses languish;
Hospitals, and groans of anguish.

Arts and sciences bewailing;
Commerce drooping, credit failing;
Placemen mocking subjects loyal;
Separations, weddings royal.

Authors who can't earn a dinner;
Many a subtle rogue a winner;
Fugitives for shelter seeking;
Misers hoarding, tradesmen breaking.

Taste and talents quite deserted;
All the laws of truth perverted;
Arrogance o'er merit soaring;
Merit silently deploring.

Ladies gambling night and morning;
Fools the works of genius scorning;

Ancient dames for girls mistaken,
Youthful damsels quite forsaken.

Some in luxury delighting;
More in talking than in fighting,
Lovers old, and beaux decrepit;
Lordlings empty and insipid.

Poets, painters, and musicians;
Lawyers, doctors, politicians;
Pamphlets, newspapers, and odes,
Seeking fame by different roads.

Gallant souls with empty purses,
Generals only fit for nurses;
School-boys, smit with martial spirit,
Taking place of veteran merit.

Honest men who can't get places,
Knaves who show unblushing faces;
Ruin hastened, peace retarded;
Candor spurned, and art rewarded.

(1795)

[79]

The Rights of Woman

Yes, injured Woman! rise, assert thy right!
Woman! too long degraded, scorned, oppressed;
Oh! born to rule in partial law's despite,
Resume thy native empire o'er the breast!

Go forth arrayed in panoply divine,
That angel pureness which admits no stain.
Go, bid proud Man his boasted rule resign
And kiss the golden sceptre of thy reign.

Go, gird thyself with grace, collect thy store
Of bright artillery glancing from afar;
Soft melting tones thy thundering cannon's roar,
Blushes and fears thy magazine of war.

Thy rights are empire; urge no meaner claim, –
Felt, not defined, and, if debated, lost,
Like sacred mysteries, which withheld from fame,
Shunning discussion, are revered the most.

Try all that wit and art suggest to bend
Of thy imperial foe the stubborn knee;
Make treacherous Man thy subject, not thy friend;
Thou mayst command, but never canst be free.

Awe the licentious and restrain the rude;
Soften the sullen, clear the cloudy brow:
Be, more than princes' gifts, thy favours sued; –
She hazards all, who will the least allow.

But hope not, courted idol of mankind,
On this proud eminence secure to stay;

Subduing and subdued, thou soon shalt find
Thy coldness soften, and thy pride give way.

Then, then abandon each ambitious thought;
Conquest or rule thy heart shall feebly move,
In Nature's school, but her soft maxims taught
That separate rights are lost in mutual love.

(1795)

Casabianca

The boy stood on the burning deck
   Whence all but he had fled;
The flame that lit the battle's wreck
   Shone round him o'er the dead.

Yet beautiful and bright he stood,
   As born to rule the storm –
A creature of heroic blood,
   A proud though childlike form.

The flames rolled on – he would not go
   Without his father's word;
That father, faint in death below,
   His voice no longer heard.

He called aloud: – 'Say, father, say
   If yet my task is done!'
He knew not that the chieftain lay
   Unconscious of his son.

'Speak, father!' once again he cried,
   'If I may yet be gone!'
And but the booming shots replied,
   And fast the flames rolled on.

Upon his brow he felt their breath,
   And in his waving hair,
And looked from that lone post of death
   In still, yet brave despair;

And shouted yet once more aloud,
   'My father! must I stay?'

While o'er him fast, through sail and shroud,
  The wreathing fires made way.

They wrapped the ship in splendour wild,
  They caught the flag on high,
And streamed above that gallant child
  Like banners in the sky.

There came a burst of thunder-sound –
  The boy – Oh! where was he?
Ask of the winds that far around
  With fragments strewed the sea! –

With mast, and helm, and pennon fair,
  That well had borne their part;
But the noblest thing which perished there
  Was that young faithful heart.

(printed 1829)

Young Casabianca, a boy about thirteen years old, son to the Admiral of the Orient, remained at his post (in the Battle of the Nile) after the ship had taken fire, and all the guns had been abandoned; and perished in the explosion of the vessel, when the flames had reached the powder.

Mary had a little lamb,
    Its fleece was white as snow;
And everywhere that Mary went
    The lamb was sure to go.

It followed her to school one day,
    That was against the rule;
It made the children laugh and play
    To see a lamb at school.

And so the teacher turned it out,
    But still it lingered near,
And waited patiently about
    Till Mary did appear.

'Why does the lamb love Mary so?'
    The eager children cry;
'Why, Mary loves the lamb, you know,'
    The teacher did reply.

   (1830)

Thoughts on my sick-bed

And has the remnant of my life
Been pilfered of this sunny spring?
And have its own prelusive sounds
Touched in my heart no echoing string?

Ah! say not so! The hidden life
Couchant within this feeble frame
Hath been enriched by kindred gifts,
That, undesired, unsought-for, came.

With joyful heart in youthful days,
When each fresh season in its round
I welcomed the earliest celandine
Glittering upon the mossy ground.

With busy eyes I pierced the lane,
In quest of known and unknown things,
The primrose a lamp on its fortress rock,
The silent butterfly spreading its wings,

The violet betrayed by its noiseless breath,
The daffodil dancing in the breeze,
The carolling thrush, on his naked perch,
Towering above the naked trees.

Our cottage-hearth no longer our home,
Companions of nature were we,
The stirring, the still, the loquacious, the mute –
To all we gave our sympathy.

Yet never in those careless days
When spring-time in rock, field, or bower

[85]

Was but a fountain of earthly hope,
A promise of fruits and the splendid flower,

No! then I never felt a bliss
That might with that compare
Which piercing to my couch of rest,
Came on the vernal air.

When loving friends an offering brought,
The first flowers of the year,
Culled from the precincts of our home,
From nooks to memory dear.

With some sad thoughts the work was done,
Unprompted and unbidden,
But joy it brought to my hidden life,
To consciousness no longer hidden.

I felt a power unfelt before,
Controlling weakness, languor, pain.
It bore me to the terrace walk –
I trod the hills again.

No prisoner in this lonely room,
I saw the green banks of the Wye,
Recalling thy prophetic words,
Bard, brother, friend from infancy!

No need of motion, or of strength,
Or even the breathing air:
 I thought of Nature's loveliest scenes,
And with memory I was there.

(1832)

Lines of Life

Orphan in my first years, I early learnt
To make my heart suffice itself, and seek
Support and sympathy in its own depth*s.*

Well, read my cheek, and watch my eye, –
    Too strictly schooled are they,
One secret of my soul to show,
    One hidden thought betray.

I never knew the time my heart
    Looked freely from my brow;
It once was checked by timidness,
    'Tis taught by caution now.

I live amongst the cold, the false,
    And I must seem like them;
And such I am, for I am false
    As those I most condemn.

I teach my lip its sweetest smile,
    My tongue its softest tone;
I borrow others' likeness, till
    Almost I lose my own.

I pass through flattery's gilded sieve
    Whatever I would say;
In social life all, like the blind,
    Must learn to feel their way.

I check my thoughts like curbéd steeds
    That struggle with the rein;
I bid my feelings sleep, like wrecks
    In the unfathomed main.

I hear them speak of love, the deep,
    The true, and mock the name;
Mock at all high and early truth,
    And I too do the same.

I hear them tell some touching tale,
    I swallow down the tear;
I hear them name some generous deed,
    And I have learnt to sneer.

I hear the spiritual, the kind,
    The pure, but named in mirth,
Till all of good, ay, even hope,
    Seems exiled from our earth.

And one fear, withering ridicule,
    Is all that I can dread,
A sword hung by a single hair
    For ever o'er the head.

We bow to a most servile faith,
    In a most servile fear,
While none among us dares to say
    What none will choose to hear.

And if we dream of loftier thoughts,
    In weakness they are gone,
And indolence and vanity
    Rivet our fetters on.

Surely I was not born for this!
    I feel a loftier mood
Of generous impulse, high resolve,
    Steal o'er my solitude!

I gaze upon the thousand stars
    That fill the midnight sky,
And wish, so passionately wish,
    A light like theirs on high.

I have such eagerness of hope
    To benefit my kind,
And feel as if immortal power
    Were given to my mind.

I think on that eternal fame,
    The sun of earthly gloom,
Which makes the gloriousness of death,
    The future of the tomb –

The earthly future, the faint sign
    Of a more heavenly one;
– A step, a word, a voice, a look –
    Alas! my dream is done!

And earth, and earth's debasing stain,
    Again is on my soul,
And I am but a nameless part
    Of a most worthless whole.

Why write I this? Because my heart
    Towards the future springs,
That future where it loves to soar
    On more than eagle wings.

The present, it is but a speck
    In that eternal time,
In which my lost hopes find a home,
    My spirit knows its clime.

Oh! not for myself, – for what am I? –
　　The worthless and the weak,
Whose every thought of self should raise
　　A blush to burn my cheek.

But song has touched my lips with fire,
　　And made my heart a shrine
For what, although alloyed, debased,
　　Is in itself divine.

I am myself but a vile link
　　Amid life's weary chain,
But I have spoken hallowed words,
　　Oh do not say in vain!

My first, my last, my only wish,
　　Say will my charméd chords
Wake to the morning light of fame
　　And breathe again my words?

Will the young maiden, when her tears
　　Alone in moonlight shine –
Tears for the absent and the loved –
　　Murmur some song of mine?

Will the pale youth by his dim lamp,
　　Himself a dying flame,
From many an antique scroll beside,
　　Choose that which bears my name?

Let music make less terrible
　　The silence of the dead;
I care not, so my spirit last
　　Long after life has fled.

　　(1829)

CHARLOTTE BRONTË

He Saw My Heart's Woe

He saw my heart's woe, discovered my soul's anguish,
　　How in fever, in thirst, in atrophy it pined,
Knew he could heal, yet looked and let it languish,
　　To its moans spirit-deaf, to its pangs spirit-blind.

But once a year he heard a whisper low and dreary,
　　Appealing for aid, entreating some reply.
Only when sick, soul-worn and torture-weary,
　　Breathed I that prayer – heaved I that sigh.

He was mute as is the grave, he stood stirless as a tower.
　　At last I looked up, and saw I prayed to stone.
I asked help of that which to help had no power,
　　I sought love where love was utterly unknown.

Idolater, I kneeled to an idol cut in rock;
　　I might have slashed my flesh and drawn my heart's best
　　　blood.
The Granite God had felt no tenderness, no shock;
　　My Baal had not seen nor heard nor understood.

In dark remorse I rose. I rose in darker shame;
　　Self-condemnéd I withdrew to an exile from my kind.
A solitude I sought where mortal never came,
　　Hoping in its wilds forgetfulness to find.

Now, Heaven, heal the wound which I still deeply feel.
　　Thy glorious hosts look not in scorn on our poor race;
Thy King eternal doth no iron judgment deal
　　On suffering worms who seek forgiveness, comfort, grace.

He gave our hearts to love, he will not love despise,
　　E'en if the gift be lost, as mine was long ago.
He will forgive the fault, will bid the offender rise,
　　Wash out with dews of bliss the fiery brand of woe,

And give a sheltered place beneath the unsullied throne,
Whence the soul redeemed may mark Time's fleeting course
　　　round earth,
And know, its trial overpast, its sufferings are gone,
And feel the peril past of Death's immortal birth.

　(1847–8)

Often rebuked, yet always back returning
To those first feelings that were born with me,
And leaving busy chase of wealth and learning
For idle dreams of things which cannot be,

Today I will seek not the shadowy region.
Its unsustaining vastness waxes drear
And visions rising, legion after legion,
Bring the unreal world too strangely near.

I'll walk, but not in old heroic traces,
And not in paths of high morality,
And not among the half-distinguished faces,
The clouded forms of long-past history.

I'll walk where my own nature would be leading –
It vexes me to choose another guide –
Where the gray flocks in ferny glens are feeding,
Where the wild wind blows on the mountain side.

What have those lonely mountains worth revealing?
More glory and more grief than I can tell.
The earth that wakes *one* human heart to feeling
Can centre both the worlds of Heaven and Hell.

(before 1848)

The Convent Threshold

There's blood between us, love, my love,
There's father's blood, there's brother's blood,
And blood's a bar I cannot pass.
I choose the stairs that mount above,
Stair after golden skyward stair,
To city and to sea of glass.
My lily feet are soiled with mud,
With scarlet mud which tells a tale
Of hope that was, of guilt that was,
Of love that shall not yet avail;
Alas, my heart, if I could bare
My heart, this selfsame stain is there:
I seek the sea of glass and fire
To wash the spot, to burn the snare;
Lo, stairs are meant to lift us higher:
Mount with me, mount the kindled stair.

Your eyes look earthward, mine look up.
I see the far-off city grand,
Beyond the hills a watered land,
Beyond the gulf a gleaming strand
Of mansions where the righteous sup,
Who sleep at ease among their trees,
Or wake to sing a cadenced hymn
With Cherubim and Seraphim.
They bore the Cross, they drained the cup,
Racked, roasted, crushed, wrenched limb from limb.
They, the offscouring of the world,
The heaven of starry heavens unfurled;
The sun before their face is dim.

You looking earthwards, what see you?
Milk-white, wine-flushed among the vines,
Up and down leaping, to and fro,
Most glad, most full, made strong with wines,
Blooming as peaches pearled with dew,
Their golden windy hair afloat,
Love-music warbling in their throat,
Young men and women come and go.

You linger, yet the time is short.
Flee for your life, gird up your strength
To flee; the shadows stretched at length
Show that day wanes, that night draws nigh.
Flee to the mountain, tarry not.
Is this a time for smile and sigh,
For songs among the secret trees
Where sudden blue birds nest and sport?
The time is short and yet you stay.
Today, while it is called today,
Kneel, wrestle, knock, do violence, pray.
To-day is short, to-morrow nigh;
Why will you die? why will you die?

You sinned with me a pleasant sin:
Repent with me, for I repent.
Woe's me the lore I must unlearn!
Woe's me that easy way we went,
So rugged when I would return!
How long until my sleep begin,
How long shall stretch these nights and days?
Surely, clean Angels cry, she prays;
She laves her soul with tedious tears:
How long must stretch these years and years?

I turn from you my cheeks and eyes,
My hair which you shall see no more –
Alas for joy that went before,
For joy that dies, for love that dies!
Only my lips still turn to you,
My livid lips that cry, Repent!
Oh weary life, Oh weary Lent,
Oh weary time whose stars are few.

How should I rest in Paradise,
Or sit on steps of heaven alone?
If Saints and Angels spoke of love
Should I not answer from my throne,
'Have pity upon me, ye my friends,
For I have heard the sound thereof'?
Should I not turn with yearning eyes,
Turn earthwards with a pitiful pang?
Oh save me from a pang in heaven.
By all the gifts we took and gave,
Repent, repent, and be forgiven.
This life is long, but yet it ends;
Repent and purge your soul and save.
No gladder song the morning stars
Upon their birthday morning sang
Than Angels sing when one repents.

I tell you what I dreamed last night:
A spirit with transfigured face
Fire-footed clomb an infinite space.
I heard his hundred pinions clang,
Heaven-bells rejoicing rang and rang,
Heaven-air was thrilled with subtle scents,
Worlds spun upon their rushing cars:
He mounted shrieking, 'Give me light!'

Still light was poured on him, more light.
Angels, Archangels he outstripped,
Exultant in exceeding might,
And trod the skirts of Cherubim.
Still 'Give me light,' he shrieked; and dipped
His thirsty face, and drank a sea,
Athirst with thirst it could not slake.
I saw him, drunk with knowledge, take
From aching brows the aureole crown –
His locks writhe like a cloven snake –
He left his throne to grovel down
And lick the dust of Seraphs' feet,
For what is knowledge duly weighed?
Knowledge is strong, but love is sweet.
Yea, all the progress he had made
Was but to learn that all is small
Save love, for love is all in all.

I tell you what I dreamed last night:
It was not dark, it was not light,
Cold dews had drenched my plenteous hair
Through clay. You came to seek me there.
And 'Do you dream of me?' you said.
My heart was dust that used to leap
To you; I answered half asleep,
'My pillow is damp, my sheets are red,
There's a leaden tester to my bed.
Find you a warmer playfellow,
A warmer pillow for your head,
A kinder love to love than mine.'
You wrung your hands: while I like lead
Crushed downwards through the sodden earth:

[97]

You smote your hands but not in mirth,
And reeled but were not drunk with wine.

For all night long I dreamed of you.
I woke and prayed against my will,
Then slept to dream of you again.
At length I rose and knelt and prayed;
I cannot write the words I said.
My words were slow, my tears were few,
But through the dark my silence spoke
Like thunder. When this morning broke,
My face was pinched, my hair was grey,
And frozen blood was on the sill
Where stifling in my struggle I lay.

If now you saw me you would say,
'Where is the face I used to love?'
And I would answer, 'Gone before.
It tarries veiled in Paradise.'
When once the morning star shall rise,
When earth with shadow flees away
And we stand safe within the door,
Then you shall lift the veil thereof.
Look up, rise up, for far above
Our palms are grown, our place is set.
There we shall meet as once we met
And love with old familiar love.

(1858)

My Heart and I

Enough! we're tired, my heart and I.
　　We sit beside the headstone thus,
　　And wish that name were carved for us.
The moss reprints more tenderly
　　The hard types of a mason's knife,
　　As Heaven's sweet life renews earth's life
With which we're tired, my heart and I.

You see, we're tired, my heart and I.
　　We dealt with books, we trusted men,
　　And in our own blood drenched the pen,
As if such colours could not fly.
　　We walked too straight for fortune's end,
　　We loved too true to keep a friend;
At last we're tired, my heart and I.

How tired we feel, my heart and I!
　　We seem of no use in the world;
　　Our fancies hang grey and uncurled
About men's eyes indifferently.
　　Our voice which thrilled you so, will let
　　You sleep; our tears are only wet.
What do we here, my heart and I?

So tired, so tired, my heart and I!
　　It was not thus in that old time
　　When Ralph sate with me 'neath the lime
To watch the sunset from the sky.
　　'Dear love, you're looking tired,' he said.
　　I, smiling at him, shook my head.
'Tis now we're tired, my heart and I.

So tired, so tired, my heart and I!
    Though now none takes me on his arm
    To fold me close and kiss me warm
Till each quick breath end in a sigh
    Of happy languor. Now, alone,
    We lean upon this graveyard stone,
Uncheered, unkissed, my heart and I.

Tired out we are, my heart and I.
    Suppose the world brought diadems
    To tempt us, crusted with loose gems
Of powers and pleasures? Let it try.
    We scarcely care to look at even
    A pretty child, or God's blue heaven,
We feel so tired, my heart and I.

Yet who complains? My heart and I!
    In this abundant earth no doubt
    Is little room for things worn out.
Disdain them, break them, throw them by,
    And if, before the days grew rough,
    We *once* were loved, used, – well enough,
I think, we've fared, my heart and I.

    (*c.*1860)

The Soul has Bandaged moments –
When too appalled to stir –
She feels some ghastly Fright come up
And stop to look at her –

Salute her – with long fingers –
Caress her freezing hair –
Sip, Goblin, from the very lips
The Lover – hovered – o'er –
Unworthy, that a thought so mean
Accost a Theme – so – fair –

The soul has moments of Escape –
When bursting all the doors –
She dances like a Bomb, abroad,
And swings upon the Hours,

As do the Bee – delirious borne –
Long Dungeoned from his Rose –
Touch Liberty – then know no more,
But Noon, and Paradise –

The Soul's retaken moments –
When, Felon led along,
With shackles on the plumed feet,
And staples, in the Song,

The Horror welcomes her, again,
These, are not brayed of Tongue –

(c.1862)

Battle-Hymn of the Republic

Mine eyes have seen the glory of the coming of the Lord:
He is trampling out the vintage where the grapes of wrath
    are stored;
He hath loosed the fateful lightning of His terrible swift sword:
      His truth is marching on.

I have seen Him in the watch-fires of a hundred circling camps;
They have builded Him an altar in the evening dews and
    damps;
I can read His righteous sentence by the dim and flaring lamps:
      His day is marching on.

I have read a fiery gospel, writ in burnished rows of steel:
'As ye deal with My contemners, so with you My grace shall
    deal;
Let the Hero, born of woman, crush the serpent with his heel,
      Since God is marching on.'

He has sounded forth the trumpet that shall never call retreat;
He is shifting out the hearts of men before His judgment-seat:
O, be swift, my soul, to answer Him! be jubilant my feet!
      Our God is marching on.

In the beauty of the lilies Christ was born across the sea,
With a glory in His bosom that transfigures you and me:
As He died to make men holy, let us die to make men free,
      While God is marching on.

(1862)

A Clever Woman

You thought I had the strength of men
   Because with men I dared to speak,
And courted Science now and then,
   And studied Latin for a week;
But woman's woman even when
   She reads her Ethics in the Greek.

You thought me wiser than my kind;
   You thought me 'more than common tall;'
You thought because I had a mind,
   That I could have no heart at all;
But woman's woman you will find,
   Whether she be great or small.

And then you needs must die – ah, well!
   I knew you not, you loved not me.
'Twas not because that darkness fell,
   You saw not what there was to see.
But I that saw and could not tell –
   O evil Angel, set me free!

   (1883)

The Mother's Charge

She raised her head. With hot and glittering eye,
'I know,' she said, 'that I am going to die.
Come here, my daughter, while my mind is clear.
Let me make plain to you your duty here;
My duty once – I never failed to try –
But for some reason I am going to die.'
She raised her head, and, while her eyes rolled wild,
Poured these instructions on the gasping child:
'Begin at once – don't iron sitting down –
Wash your potatoes when the fat is brown –
Monday, unless it rains – it always pays
To get fall sewing done on the right days –
A carpet-sweeper and a little broom –
Save dishes – wash the summer dining room
With soda – keep the children out of doors –
The starch is out – beeswax on all the floors –
If girls are treated like your friends they stay –
They stay, and treat you like their friends – the way
To make home happy is to keep a jar –
And save the prettiest pieces for the star
In the middle – blue's too dark – all silk is best –
And don't forget the corners – when they're dressed
Put them on ice – and always wash the chest
Three times a day, the windows every week –
We need more flour – the bedroom ceilings leak –
It's better than onion – keep the boys at home –
Gardening is good – a load, three loads of loam –
They bloom in spring – and smile, smile always, dear –
Be brave, keep on – I hope I've made it clear.'

She died, as all her mothers died before.
Her daughter died in turn, and made one more.

(printed 1894)

Parentage

'When Augustus Cæsar legislated against the unmarried citizens of
Rome, he declared them to be, in some sort, the slayers of the people.'

Ah no! not these!
These, who were childless, are not they who gave
So many dead unto the journeying wave,
The helpless nurslings of the cradling seas;
Not they who doomed by infallible decrees
Unnumbered man to the innumerable grave.

But those who slay
Are fathers. Theirs are armies. Death is theirs –
The death of innocences and despairs;
The dying of the golden and the grey.
The sentence, when these speak it, has no Nay.
And she who slays is she who bears, who bears.

(printed 1896)

The Quiet House

When we were children old Nurse used to say,
 The house was like an auction or a fair
 Until the lot of us were safe in bed.
 It has been quiet as the country-side
 Since Ted and Janey and then Mother died
And Tom crossed Father and was sent away.
After the lawsuit he could not hold up his head,
 Poor Father, and he does not care
 For people here, or to go anywhere.

To get away to Aunt's for that week-end
 Was hard enough; (since then, a year ago,
 He scarcely lets me slip out of his sight –)
At first I did not like my cousin's friend,
 I did not think I should remember him:
 His voice has gone, his face is growing dim
And if I like him now I do not know.
 He frightened me before he smiled –
 He did not ask me if he might –
 He said that he would come one Sunday night,
 He spoke to me as if I were a child.

No year has been like this that has just gone by;
 It may be that what Father says is true,
If things are so it does not matter why:
 But everything has burned, and not quite through.
 The colours of the world have turned
 To flame, the blue, the gold has burned
In what used to be such a leaden sky.
When you are burned quite through you die.

Red is the strangest pain to bear;
In Spring the leaves on the budding trees;
In Summer the roses are worse than these,
　　More terrible than they are sweet:
　　A rose can stab you across the street
　　　　Deeper than any knife:
　　And the crimson haunts you everywhere –
Thin shafts of sunlight, like the ghosts of reddened
　　　　　　　　swords have struck our stair
As if, coming down, you had spilt your life.

　　I think that my soul is red
Like the soul of a sword or a scarlet flower:
　　　　But when these are dead
　　　　They have had their hour.

　　　　I shall have had mine, too,
　　　　　　For from head to feet,
　　　　I am burned and stabbed half through,
　　　　　　And the pain is deadly sweet.

　　　　The things that kill us seem
　　　　　　Blind to the death they give:
　　　　It is only in our dream
　　　　　　The things that kill us live.

The room is shut where Mother died,
　　The other rooms are as they were,
The world goes on the same outside,
　　The sparrows fly across the Square,
　　The children play as we four did there,
　　The trees grow green and brown and bare,
The sun shines on the dead Church spire,
　　And nothing lives here but the fire,

While Father watches from his chair
              Day follows day
The same, or now and then, a different grey,
              Till, like his hair,
Which Mother said was wavy once and bright,
              They will all turn white.

    To-night I heard a bell again –
Outside it was the same mist of fine rain,
The lamps just lighted down the long, dim street,
              No one for me –
    I think it is myself I go to meet:
I do not care; some day I *shall* not think; I shall not *be*!

   (1913)

Song Making

My heart cries like a beaten child,
    Ceaselessly, all night long;
And I must take my own heart cries
    And thread them neatly into a song.

My heart cries like a beaten child,
    And I must listen, stark and terse,
Dry-eyed and critical, to see
    What I can turn into a verse.

This was a sob at the hour of three,
    And this when the first cock crew –
I wove them into a dainty song,
    But no-one thought it true!

(1916)

The Fired Pot

In our town, people live in rows.
The only irregular thing in a street is the steeple,
And where that points to, God only knows,
And not the poor disciplined people!

And I have watched the women growing old,
Passionate about pins, and pence, and soap,
Till the heart within my wedded breast grew cold,
And I lost hope.

But a young soldier came to our town,
He spoke his mind most candidly.
He asked me quickly to lie down,
And that was very good for me.

For though I gave him no embrace –
Remembering my duty –
He altered the expression of my face,
And gave me back my beauty.

(1916)

Full Moon

She was wearing coral taffeta trousers
Someone had bought her from Isfahan,
And the little gold coat with pomegranate blossoms,
And the coral-hafted feather fan,
But she ran down a Kentish lane in the moonlight,
And skipped in the pool of moon as she ran.

She cared not a rap for all the big planets,
For Betelgeuse or Aldebaran,
And all the big planets cared nothing for her,
That small impertinent charlatan,
As she climbed on a Kentish stile in the moonlight,
And laughed at the sky through the sticks of her fan.

(1921)

The Sisters

Taking us by and large, we're a queer lot
We women who write poetry. And when you think
How few of us there've been, it's queerer still.
I wonder what it is that makes us do it,
Singles us out to scribble down, man-wise,
The fragments of ourselves. Why are we
Already mother-creatures, double-bearing,
With matrices in body and in brain?
I rather think that there is just the reason
We are so sparse a kind of human being;
The strength of forty thousand Atlases
Is needed for our everyday concerns.
There's Sappho, now I wonder what was Sappho.
I know a single slender thing about her:
That, loving, she was like a burning birch-tree
All tall and glittering fire, and that she wrote
Like the same fire caught up to Heaven and held there,
A frozen blaze before it broke and fell.
Ah, me! I wish I could have talked to Sappho,
Surprised her reticences by flinging mine
Into the wind. This tossing off of garments
Which cloud the soul is none too easy doing
With us today. But still I think with Sappho
One might accomplish it, were she in the mood
To bare her loveliness of words and tell
The reasons, as she possibly conceived them,
Of why they are so lovely. Just to know
How she came at them, just to watch
The crisp sea sunshine playing on her hair,

And listen, thinking all the while 'twas she
Who spoke and that we two were sisters
Of a strange, isolated little family.
And she is Sappho – Sappho – not Miss or Mrs,
A leaping fire we call so for convenience;
But Mrs Browning – who would ever think
Of such a presumption as to call her 'Ba.'
Which draws the perfect line between sea-cliffs
And a close-shuttered room in Wimpole Street.
Sappho could fly her impulses like bright
Balloons tip-tilting to a morning air
And write about it. Mrs Browning's heart
Was squeezed in stiff conventions. So she lay
Stretched out upon a sofa, reading Greek
And speculating, as I must suppose,
In just this way on Sappho; all the need,
The huge, imperious need of loving, crushed
Within the body she believed so sick.
And it was sick, poor lady, because words
Are merely simulacra after deeds
Have wrought a pattern; when they take the place
Of actions they breed a poisonous miasma
Which, though it leave the brain, eats up the body.
So Mrs Browning, aloof and delicate,
Lay still upon her sofa, all her strength
Going to uphold her over-topping brain.
It seems miraculous, but she escaped
To freedom and another motherhood
Than that of poems. She was a very woman
And needed both.
                    If I had gone to call,
Would Wimpole Street have been the kindlier place,
Or Casa Guidi, in which to have met her?

I am a little doubtful of that meeting,
For Queen Victoria was very young and strong
And all-pervading in her apogee
At just that time. If we had stuck to poetry,
Sternly refusing to be drawn off by mesmerism
Or Roman revolutions, it might have done.
For, after all, she is another sister,
But always, I rather think, an older sister
And not herself so curious a technician
As to admit newfangled modes of writing –
'Except, of course, in Robert, and that is neither
Here nor there for Robert is a genius.'
I do not like the turn this dream is taking,
Since I am very fond of Mrs Browning
And very much indeed should like to hear her
Graciously asking me to call her 'Ba.'
But then the Devil of Verisimilitude
Creeps in and forces me to know she wouldn't.
Convention again, and how it chafes my nerves,
For we are such a little family
Of singing sisters, and as if I didn't know
What those years felt like tied down to the sofa.
Confound Victoria, and the slimy inhibitions
She loosed on all us Anglo-Saxon creatures!
Suppose there hadn't been a Robert Browning,
No *Sonnets from the Portuguese* would have been written.
They are the first of all her poems to be,
One might say, fertilised. For, after all,
A poet is flesh and blood as well as brain
And Mrs Browning, as I said before,
Was very, very woman. Well, there are two
Of us, and vastly unlike that's for certain,
Unlike at least until we tear the veils

Away which commonly gird our souls. I scarcely think
Mrs Browning would have approved the process
In spite of what had surely been relief;
For speaking souls must always want to speak
Even when bat-eyed, narrow-minded Queens
Set prudishness to keep the keys of impulse.
Then do the frowning Gods invent new banes
And make the need of sofas. But Sappho was dead
And I, and others, not yet peeped above
The edge of possibility. So that's an end
To speculating over tea-time talks
Beyond the movement of pentameters
With Mrs Browning.
                         But I go dreaming on,
In love with these my spiritual relations.
I rather think I see myself walk up
A flight of wooden steps and ring a bell
And send a card in to Miss Dickinson.
Yet that's a very silly way to do.
I should have taken the dream twist-ends about
And climbed over the fence and found her deep
Engrossed in the doings of a humming-bird
Among nasturtiums. Not having expected strangers,
She might forget to think me one, and holding up
A finger say quite casually: 'Take care.
Don't frighten him, he's only just begun.'
'Now this,' I well believe I should have thought,
'Is even better than Sappho. With Emily
You're really here, or never anywhere at all
In range of mind.' Wherefore, having begun
In the strict centre we could slowly progress
To various circumferences, as we pleased.
We could, but should we? That would quite depend

On Emily. I think she'd be exacting,
Without intention possibly, and ask
A thousand tight-rope tricks of understanding.
But, bless you, I would somersault all day
If by doing so I might stay with her.
I hardly think that we should mention souls
Although they might just round the corner from us
In some half-quizzical, half-wistful metaphor.
I'm very sure that I should never seek
To turn her parables to stated fact.
Sapho would speak, I think, quite openly,
And Mrs Browning guard a careful silence,
But Emily would set doors ajar and slam them
And love you for your speed of observation.

  Strange trio of my sisters, most diverse,
  And how extraordinarily unlike
  Each is to me, and which way shall I go?
  Sappho spent and gained; and Mrs Browning,
  After a miser girlhood, cut the strings
  Which tied her money-bags and let them run;
  But Emily hoarded – hoarded – only giving
  Herself to cold, white paper. Starved and tortured,
  She cheated her despair with games of patience
  And fooled herself by winning. Frail little elf,
  The lonely brain-child of a gaunt maturity,
  She hung her womanhood upon a bough
  And played ball with the stars – too long – too long –
  The garment of herself hung on a tree
  Until at last she lost even the desire
  To take it down. Whose fault? Why let us say,
  To be consistent, Queen Victoria's.
  But really, not to over-rate the queen,

I feel obliged to mention Martin Luther,
And behind him the long line of Church Fathers
Who draped their prurience like a dirty cloth
About the naked majesty of God.
Good-bye, my sisters, all of you are great,
And all of you are marvelously strange,
And none of you has any word for me.
I cannot write like you, I cannot think
In terms of Pagan or Christian now.
I only hope that possibly some day
Some other woman with an itch for writing
May turn to me as I have turned to you
And chat with me for a brief few minutes. How
We lie, we poets! It is three good hours
I have been dreaming. Has it seemed so long
To you? And yet I thank you for the time
Although you leave me sad and self-distrustful,
For older sisters are very sobering things.
Put on your cloaks, my dears, the motor's waiting.
No, you have not seemed strange to me, but near,
Frightfully near, and rather terrifying.
I understand you all, for in myself –
Is that presumption? Yet indeed it's true –
We are one family. And still my answer
Will not be any one of yours, I see.
Well, never mind that now. Good night! Good night!

(printed 1922)

Let No Charitable Hope

Now let no charitable hope
Confuse my mind with images
Of eagle and of antelope:
I am in nature none of these.

I was, being human, born alone;
I am, being woman, hard beset;
I live by squeezing from a stone
The little nourishment I get.

In masks outrageous and austere
The years go by in single file;
But none has merited my fear,
And none has quite escaped my smile.

(1923)

EDNA ST VINCENT MILLAY

[Sonnet]

I, being born a woman and distressed
By all the needs and notions of my kind,
Am urged by your propinquity to find
Your person fair, and feel a certain zest
To bear your body's weight upon my breast:
So subtly is the fume of life designed,
To clarify the pulse and cloud the mind,
And leave me once again undone, possessed.
Think not for this, however, the poor treason
Of my stout blood against my staggering brain,
I shall remember you with love, or season
My scorn with pity, – let me make it plain:
I find this frenzy insufficient reason
For conversation when we meet again.

(1923)

The Crows

The woman who has grown old
And knows desire must die,
Yet turns to love again,
Hears the crows' cry.

She is a stem long hardened,
A weed that no scythe mows.
The heart's laughter will be to her
The crying of the crows.

Who slide in the air with the same voice
Over what yields not, and what yields,
Alike in spring, and when there is only bitter
Winter-burning in the fields.

(1923)

Four in the Morning

Cried the navy-blue ghost
Of Mr Belaker
The allegro Negro cocktail-shaker,
'Why did the cock crow?
Why am I lost,
Down the endless road to Infinity toss'd?
The tropical leaves are whispering white
As water; I race the wind in my flight.
The white lace houses are carried away
By the tide; far out they float and sway.
White is the nursemaid on the parade.
Is she real, as she flirts with me unafraid?
I raced through the leaves as white as water . . .
Ghostly, flowed over the nursemaid, caught her,
Left her . . . edging the far-off sand
Is the foam of the sirens' Metropole and Grand.
And along the parade I am blown and lost,
Down the endless road to Infinity toss'd.
The guinea-fowl-plumaged houses sleep . . .
On one, I saw the lone grass weep,
Where only the whimpering greyhound wind
Chased me, raced me, for what it could find.'
And there in the black and furry boughs
How slowly, coldly, old Time grows,
Where the pigeons smelling of gingerbread,
And the spectacled owls so deeply read,
And the sweet ring-doves of curded milk,
Watch the Infanta's gown of silk
In the ghost-room tall where the governante

Gesticulates lente, and walks andante.
'Madam, Princesses must be obedient;
For a medicine now becomes expedient, –
Of five ingredients, – a diapente,'
Said the governante, fading lente . . .
In at the window then looked he,
The navy-blue ghost of Mr Belaker,
The allegro Negro cocktail-shaker, –
And his flattened face like the moon saw she, –
Rhinoceros-black (a flowing sea!).

(1924)

H.D. (HILDA DOOLITTLE)

Fragment Thirty-six

I know not what to do: my mind is divided. – Sappho.

I know not what to do,
my mind is reft:
is song's gift best?
is love's gift loveliest?
I know not what I do,
now sleep has pressed
weight on your eyelids.

Shall I break your rest,
devouring, eager?
is love's gift best?
nay, song's the loveliest:
yet were you lost,
what rapture
could I take from song?
what song were left?

I know not what to do:
to turn and slake
the rage that burns,
with my breath burn
and trouble your cool breath?
so shall I turn and take
snow in my arms?
(is love's gift best?)
yet flake on flake
of snow were comfortless,
did you lie wondering,
wakened yet unawake.

[124]

Shall I turn and take
comfortless snow within my arms?
press lips to lips
that answer not,
press lips to flesh
that shudders not nor breaks?

Is love's gift best?
shall I turn and slake
all the wild longing?
O I am eager for you!
as the Pleiads shake
white light in whiter water
so shall I take you?

My mind is quite divided,
my minds hesitate,
so perfect matched,
I know not what to do:
each strives with each
as two white wrestlers
standing for a match,
ready to turn and clutch
yet never shake muscle nor nerve nor tendon;
so my mind waits
to grapple with my mind,
yet I lie quiet,
I would seem at rest.

I know not what to do:
strain upon strain,
sound surging upon sound
makes my brain blind;
as a wave-line may wait to fall

yet (waiting for its falling)
still the wind may take
from off its crest,
white flake on flake of foam,
that rises,
seeming to dart and pulse
and rend the light,
so my mind hesitates
above the passion
quivering yet to break,
so my mind hesitates
above my mind,
listening to song's delight.

I know not what to do:
will the sound break,
rending the night
with rift on rift of rose
and scattered light?
will the sound break at last
as the wave hesitant,
or will the whole night pass
and I lie listening awake?

(1924)

DOROTHY PARKER

Résumé

Razors pain you;
Rivers are damp;
Acids stain you;
And drugs cause cramp.
Guns aren't lawful;
Nooses give;
Gas smells awful;
You might as well live.

(printed 1926)

Poetry

I, too, dislike it: there are things that are important beyond
        all this fiddle.
  Reading it, however, with a perfect contempt for it, one
        discovers in
  it after all, a place for the genuine.
    Hands that can grasp, eyes
    that can dilate, hair that can rise
        if it must, these things are important not because a

high-sounding interpretation can be put upon them but
        because they are
  useful. When they become so derivative as to become
        unintelligible,
  the same thing may be said for all of us, that we
    do not admire what
    we cannot understand: the bat
        holding on upside down or in quest of something to

eat, elephants pushing, a wild horse taking a roll, a tireless
        wolf under
  a tree, the immovable critic twitching his skin like a horse
        that feels a flea, the base-
  ball fan, the statistician –
    nor is it valid
        to discriminate against 'business documents and

school-books'; all of these phenomena are important. One
        must make a distinction
  however: when dragged into prominence by half poets,
        the result is not poetry,
  nor till the poets among us can be

  'literalists of

  the imagination' – above

   insolence and triviality and can present

for inspection, 'imaginary gardens with real toads in them',

    shall we have

  it. In the meantime, if you demand on the one hand,

  the raw material of poetry in

   all its rawness and

   that which is on the other hand

    genuine, you are interested in poetry.

(1919, 1935)

Infelice

Walking swiftly with a dreadful duchess,
He smiled too briefly, his face was as pale as sand,
He jumped into a taxi when he saw me coming,
Leaving me alone with a private meaning,
He loves me so much, my heart is singing.
Later at the Club when I rang him in the evening
They said: Sir Rat is dining, is dining, is dining,
No Madam, he left no message, ah how his silence speaks,
He loves me too much for words, my heart is singing.
The Pullman seats are here, the tickets for Paris, I am waiting,
Presently the telephone rings, it is his valet speaking,
Sir Rat is called away, to Scotland, his constituents,
(Ah the dreadful duchess, but he loves me best)
Best pleasure to the last, my heart is singing.
One night he came, it was four in the morning,
Walking slowly upstairs, he stands beside my bed,
Dear darling, lie beside me, it is too cold to stand speaking,
He lies down beside me, his face is like the sand,
He is in a sleep of love, my heart is singing.
Sleeping softly softly, in the morning I must wake him,
And he waking murmurs, I only came to sleep.
The words so sweetly cruel, how deeply he loves me,
I say them to myself alone, my heart is singing.
Now the sunshine strengthens, it is ten in the morning,
He is so timid in love, he only needs to know,
He is my little child, how can he come if I do not call him,
I will write and tell him everything, I take the pen and write:
I love you so much, my heart is singing.

*(c.*1936)

[Sonnet]

When I have said 'I love you' I have said
Nothing at all to tell you; I cannot find
Any speech in any country of the mind
Which might inform you whither I have fled.
In saying 'I love you' I have gone so far
Away from you, into so strange a land;
You may not find me, may not understand
How I am exiled, driven to a star

Till now deserted. Here I stand about,
Eat, sleep, bewail, feel lonely and explore,
Remember how I loved the world, before,
Tremble in case that memory lets me out.
Islanded here, I wait for you to come –
Waiting the day that exiles you to home.

(1938)

Who in One Lifetime

Who in one lifetime sees all causes lost,
Herself dismayed and helpless, cities down,
Love made monotonous fear and the sad-faced
Inexorable armies and the falling plane,
Has sickness, sickness. Introspective and whole.
She knows how several madnesses are born,
Seeing the integrated never fighting well,
The flesh too vulnerable, the eyes tear-torn.

She finds a pre-surrender on all sides:
Treaty before the war, ritual impatience turn
The camps of ambush to chambers of imagery.
She holds belief in the world, she stays and hides
Life in her own defeat, stands, though her whole world burn,
A childless goddess of fertility.

(1941)

the mother

Abortions will not let you forget.
You remember the children you got that you did not get,
The damp small pulps with a little or with no hair,
The singers and workers that never handled the air.
You will never neglect or beat
Them, or silence or buy with a sweet.
You will never wind up the sucking-thumb
Or scuttle off ghosts that come.
You will never leave them, controlling your luscious sigh,
Return for a snack of them, with gobbling mother-eye.

I have heard in the voices of the wind the voices of my dim
    killed children.
I have contracted. I have eased
My dim dears at the breasts they could never suck.
I have said, Sweets, if I sinned, if I seized
Your luck
And your lives from your unfinished reach,
If I stole your births and your names,
Your straight baby tears and your games,
Your stilted or lovely loves, your tumults, your marriages,
    aches, and your deaths,
If I poisoned the beginnings of your breaths,
Believe that even in my deliberateness I was not deliberate.
Though why should I whine,
Whine that the crime was other than mine? –
Since anyhow you are dead.
Or rather, or instead,
You were never made.

But that too, I am afraid,
Is faulty: oh, what shall I say, how is the truth to be said?
You were born, you had body, you died.
It is just that you never giggled or planned or cried.

Believe me, I loved you all.
Believe me, I knew you, though faintly, and I loved, I loved
    you
All.

(printed 1945)

The Stockdove

Close in the hollow bank she lies,
Soiling with clay her azure dress:
Then slowly lifts that head, whose eyes
Have given a name to gentleness.
O is she caught, and is she snared,
Or why so still, and perched so low?
She is not ruffled, is not scared,
And yet I watch, and cannot go.

And dumbly comes the hard reply;
Death shakes her like a winter storm;
Then her round head she would put by,
As she was wont, in feathers warm:
Half lifts the wing, half turns the bill,
Then leans more lowly on the clay,
Sighs, and at last is quiet and still,
Sits there, and yet is fled away.

The epoch will not suffer me
To weep above such humble dead,
Or I could mourn a century
For all such woe unmerited:
For the soft eye, the feathers blue,
The voice more gentle than the rain,
The feet that dabbled in the dew,
We strew the field with poisoned grain.

My questioned spirit's sidelong look
From her old fortress answers me,
From where she reads her secret book
On the tall rock Infinity:

From where the innocent dead to that
High place is fled away from grief,
And whence as from an Ararat
She brings the silver olive-leaf.

(printed 1950)

He is more than a hero
(from Sappho)

He is a god in my eyes –
the man who is allowed
to sit beside you – he

who listens intimately
to the sweet murmur of
your voice, the enticing

laughter that makes my own
heart beat fast. If I meet
you suddenly, I can't

speak – my tongue is broken;
a thin flame runs under
my skin; seeing nothing,

hearing only my own ears
drumming, I drip with sweat;
trembling shakes my body

and I turn paler than
dry grass. At such times
death isn't far from me

(*c.*1950)

MAY SWENSON

The Centaur

The summer that I was ten –
Can it be there was only one
summer that I was ten? It must

have been a long one then –
each day I'd go out to choose
a fresh horse from my stable

which was a willow grove
down by the old canal.
I'd go on my two bare feet.

But when, with my brother's jack-knife,
I had cut me a long limber horse
with a good thick knob for a head,

and peeled him slick and clean
except a few leaves for the tail,
and cinched my brother's belt

around his head for a rein,
I'd straddle and canter him fast
up the grass bank to the path,

trot along in the lovely dust
that talcumed over his hoofs,
hiding my toes, and turning

his feet to swift half-moons.
The willow knob with the strap
jouncing between my thighs

[138]

was the pommel and yet the poll
of my nickering pony's head.
My head and my neck were mine,

yet they were shaped like a horse.
My hair flopped to the side
like the mane of a horse in the wind.

My forelock swung in my eyes,
my neck arched and I snorted.
I shied and skittered and reared,

stopped and raised my knees,
pawed at the ground and quivered.
My teeth bared as we wheeled

and swished through the dust again.
I was the horse and the rider,
and the leather I slapped to his rump

spanked my own behind.
Doubled, my two hoofs beat
a gallop along the bank,

the wind twanged in my mane,
my mouth squared to the bit.
And yet I sat on my steed

quiet, negligent riding,
my toes standing the stirrups,
my thighs hugging his ribs.

At a walk we drew up to the porch.
I tethered him to a paling.
Dismounting, I smoothed my skirt

and entered the dusky hall.
My feet on the clean linoleum
left ghostly toes in the hall.

Where have you been? said my mother.
Been riding, I said from the sink,
and filled me a glass of water.

What's that in your pocket? she said.
Just my knife. It weighted my pocket
and stretched my dress awry.

Go tie back your hair, said my mother,
And *Why is your mouth all green?*
*Rob Roy, he pulled some clover
as we crossed the field,* I told her.

(*1956*)

The Colossus

I shall never get you put together entirely,
Pieced, glued, and properly jointed.
Mule-bray, pig-grunt and bawdy cackles
Proceed from your great lips.
It's worse than a barnyard.

Perhaps you consider yourself an oracle,
Mouthpiece of the dead, or of some god or other.
Thirty years now I have laboured
To dredge the silt from your throat.
I am none the wiser.

Scaling little ladders with gluepots and pails of lysol
I crawl like an ant in mourning
Over the weedy acres of your brow
To mend the immense skull-plates and clear
The bald, white tumuli of your eyes.

A blue sky out of the Oresteia
Arches above us. O father, all by yourself
You are pithy and historical as the Roman Forum.
I open my lunch on a hill of black cypress.
Your fluted bones and acanthine hair are littered

In their old anarchy to the horizon-line.
It would take more than a lightning-stroke
To create such a ruin.
Nights, I squat in the cornucopia
Of your left ear, out of the wind,

Counting the red stars and those of plum-colour.
The sun rises under the pillar of your tongue.

My hours are married to shadow.
No longer do I listen for the scrape of a keel
On the blank stones of the landing.

(1959)

Woman with Girdle

Your midriff sags toward your knees;
your breasts lie down in air,
their nipples as uninvolved
as warm starfish.
You stand in your elastic case,
still not giving up the new-born
and the old-born cycle.
Moving, you roll down the garment,
down that pink snapper and hoarder,
as your belly, soft as pudding,
slops into the empty space;
down, over the surgeon's careful mark,
down over hips, those head cushions
and mouth cushions,
slow motion like a rolling pin,
over crisp hairs, that amazing field
that hides your genius from your patron;
over thighs, thick as young pigs,
over knees like saucers,
over calves, polished as leather,
down toward the feet.
You pause for a moment,
tying your ankles into knots.
Now you rise,
a city from the sea,
born long before Alexandria was,
straightway from God you have come
into your redeeming skin.

(printed 1962)

[143]

JUDITH WRIGHT

To Another Housewife

Do you remember how we went,
on duty bound, to feed the crowd
of hungry dogs your father kept
as rabbit-hunters? Lean and loud,
half-starved and furious, how they leapt
against their chains, as though they meant
in mindless rage for being fed,
to tear our childish hands instead!

With tomahawk and knife we hacked
the flyblown tatters of old meat,
gagged at their carcass-smell, and threw
the scraps and watched the hungry eat.
Then turning faint, we made a pact,
(two greensick girls), crossed hearts and swore
to touch no meat forever more.

How many cuts of choice and prime
our housewife hands have dressed since then –
these hands with love and blood imbrued –
for daughters, sons, and hungry men!
How many creatures bred for food
we've raised and fattened for the time
they met at last the steaming knife
that serves the feast of death-in-life!

And as the evening meal is served
we hear the turned-down radio
begin to tell the evening news
just as the family joint is carved.
O murder, famine, pious wars....

Our children shrink to see us so,
in sudden meditation, stand
with knife and fork in either hand.

(printed 1966)

Bad Dreams

I still have bad dreams, although
I think the worst dreams have me.
Stairs and lifts take me to awful heights
Where I hang like Harold Lloyd, or fall.
Faceless German soldiers, trailing me
From childhood, close in and bayonet me
To a death in sweating wakefulness.
I stifle in tiny Anderson shelters,
Or pick my way through the dead laid out
In familiar Shaftesbury Avenue.
Sometimes red meat confronts me bloodily,
(This one could be disgorged,
But occasional guilt is easier to bear.)

Good dreams diminish and I forget
To astonish with my abilities
To fly, or dance better than Fonteyn.
Sensual encounters grow rare
And fragments from coloured dreams
Submerge like lost tesserae.

Sometimes I recognise my terror
For the dream it is and haul myself from fear
And once, I dreamt of putting all my eggs,
But one, into one basket –
Then awoke to the grey in the window
And felt the oval solid dissolve in my hand.
But this seems small knowledge to dredge

From so much turmoil, and I don't know
That I want to prove anything anyway.

(1962–6)

No more Boomerang

No more boomerang
No more spear;
Now all civilised –
Colour bar and beer.

No more corroboree,
Gay dance and din.
Now we got movies,
And pay to go in.

No more sharing
What the hunter brings.
Now we work for money,
Then pay it back for things.

Now we track bosses,
To catch a few bob,
Then we go walkabout
On bus to the job.

One time naked,
Who never knew shame;
Now we put clothes on
To hide whatsaname.

No more gunya,
Now bungalow,
Paid by higher purchase
In twenty year or so.

Lay down the stone axe,
Take up the steel,

And work like a nigger
For a white man meal.

No more firesticks
That made the whites scoff.
Now all electric,
And no better off.

Bunyip he finish,
Now got instead
Whitefella Bunyip,
Call him Red.

Abstract picture now –
What they coming at?
Cripes, in our caves we
Did better than that.

Black hunted wallaby,
White hunt dollar;
Whitefella witch-doctor
Wear dog-collar.

No more message-stick;
Lubras and lads
Got television now,
Mostly ads.

Lay down the woomera,
Lay down the waddy,
Now we got atom-bomb,
End *every*-body.

    (printed 1981)

The Mutes

Those groans men use
passing a woman on the street
or on the steps of the subway

to tell her she is female
and their flesh knows it,

are they a sort of tune,
an ugly enough song, sung
by a bird with a slit tongue

but meant for music?

Or are they the muffled roaring
of deafmutes trapped in a building that is
slowly filling with smoke?

Perhaps both.

Such men most often
look as if groan were all they could do,
yet a woman, in spite of herself,

knows it's a tribute:
if she were lacking all grace
they'd pass her in silence:

so it's not only to say she's
a warm hole. It's a word

in grief-language, nothing to do with
primitive, not an ur-language;
language stricken, sickened, cast down

in decrepitude. She wants to
throw the tribute away, dis-
gusted, and can't,

it goes on buzzing in her ear,
it changes the pace of her walk,
the torn posters in echoing corridors

spell it out, it
quakes and gnashes as the train comes in.
Her pulse sullenly

had picked up speed,
but the cars slow down and
jar to a stop while her understanding

keeps on translating:
'Life after life after life goes by

without poetry,
without seemliness,
without love.'

   (printed 1967)

Summer Song for me and my Aunts

Never forget the moors
Behind the house, never
Let being a woman
Or the baking of bread
Or sizing up a sermon

Keep you off the heath
And far from the stone wall
That is no more than gauze
To these strong winds.
Headaches come indoors.

Walk uphill from the house
And the graves already there.
The chill of waterfalls
Cannot cause worse coughing
Than sprig-papered walls

Where you die in turn
On a narrow sofa
Boxed up from the storm.
Dying women can walk
On the moors without harm.

(printed 1967)

I felt, under my old breasts, this April day
Young breasts, like leaf and flower to come, under gray
    apple-buds
And heard a young girl within me say,
'Let me be free of this winter bark, this toil-worn body,
I who am young,
My form subtle as a dream'.
And I replied, 'You, who are I,
Entered a sad house when you put on my clay.
This shabby menial self, and life-long time,
Bear with as you may
Until your ripening joy
Put off the dust and ashes that I am,
Like winter scales cast from the living tree.'

   (printed 1971)

Against Coupling

I write in praise of the solitary act:
of not feeling a trespassing tongue
forced into one's mouth, one's breath
smothered, nipples crushed against the
ribcage, and that metallic tingling
in the chin set off by a certain odd nerve:

unpleasure. Just to avoid those eyes would help –
such eyes as a young girl draws life from,
listening to the vegetal
rustle within her, as his gaze
stirs polypal fronds in the obscure
sea-bed of her body, and her own eyes blur.

There is much to be said for abandoning
this no longer novel exercise –
for not 'participating in
a total experience' – when
one feels like the lady in Leeds who
had seen *The Sound of Music* eighty-six times;

or more, perhaps, like the school drama mistress
producing *A Midsummer Night's Dream*
for the seventh year running, with
yet another cast from 5B.
Pyramus and Thisbe are dead, but
the hole in the wall can still be troublesome.

I advise you, then, to embrace it without
encumbrance. No need to set the scene,
dress up (or undress), make speeches.

Five minutes of solitude are
enough – in the bath, or to fill
that gap between the Sunday papers and lunch.

(printed 1971)

How It Is

Shall I say how it is in your clothes?
A month after your death I wear your blue jacket.
The dog at the centre of my life recognises
you've come to visit, he's ecstatic.
In the left pocket, a hole.
In the right, a parking ticket
delivered up last August on Bay State Road.
In my heart, a scatter like milkweed,
a flinging from the pods of the soul.
My skin presses your old outline.
It is hot and dry inside.

I think of the last day of your life,
old friend, how I would unwind it, paste
it together in a different collage,
back from the death car idling in the garage,
back up the stairs, your praying hands unlaced,
reassembling the bits of bread and tuna fish
into a ceremony of sandwich,
running the home movie backward to a space
we could be easy in, a kitchen place
with vodka and ice, our words like living meat.

Dear friend, you have excited crowds
with your example. They swell
like wine bags, straining at your seams.
I will be years gathering up our words,
fishing out letters, snapshots, stains,

leaning my ribs against this durable cloth
to put on the dumb blue blazer of your death.

(*1974*)

Warning

When I am an old woman I shall wear purple
With a red hat which doesn't go, and doesn't suit me.
And I shall spend my pension on brandy and summer gloves
And satin sandals, and say we've no money for butter.
I shall sit down on the pavement when I'm tired
And gobble up samples in shops and press alarm bells
And run my stick along the public railings
And make up for the sobriety of my youth.
I shall go out in my slippers in the rain
And pick the flowers in other people's gardens
And learn to spit.

You can wear terrible shirts and grow more fat
And eat three pounds of sausages at a go
Or only bread and pickle for a week
And hoard pens and pencils and beermats and things in boxes.

But now we must have clothes that keep us dry
And pay our rent and not swear in the street
And set a good example for the children.
We must have friends to dinner and read the papers.

But maybe I ought to practise a little now?
So people who know me are not too shocked and surprised
When suddenly I am old, and start to wear purple.

(printed 1974)

Growing

Not to be passive simply, never that.
Watchful, yes, but wondering. It seems
Strange, your world, and must do always, yet
Haven't you often been caught out in dreams

And changed your terms of reference, escaped
From the long rummaging with words, with things,
Then found the very purpose that you mapped
Has moved? The poem leaves you and it sings.

And you have changed. Your whispered world is not
Yours any longer. It's not there you grow.
I tell you that your flowers will find no plot

Except when you have left them free and slow,
While you attend to other things. Do not
Tamper with touching. Others pick, you know.

(printed 1975)

One Art

The art of losing isn't hard to master;
so many things seem filled with the intent
to be lost that their loss is no disaster.

Lose something every day. Accept the fluster
of lost door keys, the hour badly spent.
The art of losing isn't hard to master.

Then practice losing farther, losing faster:
places, and names and where it was you meant
to travel. None of these will bring disaster.

I lost my mother's watch. And look! my last, or
next-to-last, of three loved houses went.
The art of losing isn't hard to master.

I lost two cities, lovely ones. And, vaster,
some realms I owned, two rivers, a continent.
I miss them, but it wasn't a disaster.

– Even losing you (the joking voice, a gesture
I love) I shan't have lied. It's evident
the art of losing's not too hard to master
though it may look like (*Write* it!) like disaster.

(printed 1976)

The Photos

My sister in her well-tailored silk blouse hands me
the photo of my father
in naval uniform and white hat.
I say, 'Oh, this is the one which Mama used to have on her
    dresser.'

My sister controls her face and furtively looks at my mother,
a sad rag bag of a woman, lumpy and sagging everywhere,
like a mattress at the Salvation Army, though with no holes
    or tears,
and says, 'No.'

I look again,
and see that my father is wearing a wedding ring,
which he never did
when he lived with my mother. And that there is a legend
    on it,
'To my dearest wife,
    Love
    Chief'
And I realise the photo must have belonged to his second
    wife,
whom he left our mother to marry.

My mother says, with her face as still as the whole
    unpopulated part of the state of North Dakota,
'May I see it too?'
She looks at it.

I look at my tailored sister
and my own blue-jeaned self. Have we wanted to hurt our
    mother,
sharing these pictures on this, one of the few days I ever visit or
spend with family? For her face is curiously haunted,
not now with her usual viperish bitterness,
but with something so deep it could not be spoken.

I turn away and say I must go on, as I have a dinner
    engagement with friends.
But I drive all the way to Pasadena from Whittier,
thinking of my mother's face; how I could never love her;
    how my father
could not love her either. Yet knowing I have inherited
the rag-bag body,
stony face with bulldog jaws.

I drive, thinking of that face.
Jeffers' California Medea who inspired me to poetry.
I killed my children,
but there as I am changing lanes on the freeway,
    necessarily glancing in the rearview mirror, I see the face,
not even a ghost, but always with me, like a photo in a
    beloved's wallet.

How I hate my destiny.

  (1976)

AUDRE LORDE

On a Night of the Full Moon

i

Out of my flesh that hungers
and my mouth that knows
comes the shape I am seeking
for reason.
The curve of your waiting body
fits my waiting hand
your breasts warm as sunlight
your lips as quick as young birds
between your thighs the sweet
sharp taste of limes.

Thus I hold you
frank in my heart's eye
in my skin's knowing
as my fingers conceive your flesh
I feel your stomach
moving against me.

Before the moon wanes again
we shall come together.

ii

And I would be the moon
spoken over your beckoning flesh
breaking against reservations
beaching thought
my hands at your high tide
over and under inside you

and the passing of hungers
attended, forgotten.

Darkly risen
the moon speaks
my eyes
judging your roundness
delightful.

 (1976)

Thoughts After Ruskin

Women reminded him of lilies and roses.
Me they remind rather of blood and soap,
Armed with a warm rag, assaulting noses,
Ears, neck, mouth and all the secret places:

Armed with a sharp knife, cutting up liver,
Holding hearts to bleed under a running tap,
Gutting and stuffing, pickling and preserving,
Scalding, blanching, broiling, pulverising,
– All the terrible chemistry of their kitchens.

Their distant husbands lean across mahogany
And delicately manipulate the market,
While safe at home, the tender and the gentle
Are killing tiny mice, dead snap by the neck,
Asphyxiating flies, evicting spiders,
Scrubbing, scouring aloud, disturbing cupboards,
Committing things to dustbins, twisting, wringing,
Wrists red and knuckles white and fingers puckered,
Pulpy, tepid. Steering screaming cleaners
Around the snags of furniture, they straighten
And haul out sheets from under the incontinent
And heavy old, stoop to importunate young,
Tugging, folding, tucking, zipping, buttoning,
Spooning in food, encouraging excretion,
Mopping up vomit, stabbing cloth with needles,
Contorting wool around their knitting needles,
Creating snug and comfy on their needles.

Their huge hands! their everywhere eyes! their voices
Raised to convey across the hullabaloo,

Their massive thighs and breasts dispensing comfort,
Their bloody passages and hairy crannies,
Their wombs that pocket a man upside down!
And when all's over, off with overalls,
Quickly consulting clocks, they go upstairs,
Sit and sigh a little, brushing hair,
And somehow find, in mirrors, colours, odours,
Their essences of lilies and of roses.

(printed 1976)

Only a Small Death

Only a small death, of course,
Not the full ceremony with mourners, a hearse,
Residuary legatees and a beanfeast
After the crematorium. Just a small, fully-
Conscious end.

Never again will you sleep in
This room, see the sun rise through glass at this
Familiar angle, never again
Adjust to the shape of this bath, the smell
Of this cupboard.

You have died suddenly. The arrival
Of undertakers informs you of your
Decease. Their muscular detachment dissolves
Bonds between chairs and rooms, shelves
And their books.

The house offers its own valuation
Of the late owner. Dirt appears
In embarrassing contexts. If you were still
Alive, you would feel the need
To apologise.

Casual adjuncts of ordinary
Living, dustbins and drains, the
Unremarkable milkman, haloed in
The otherworldly glare of the last rites,
Achieve reality

Just as you end with them for ever.
Neighbours, paying a deathbed visit,

Acquire the tender resonance of friends,
But die as you go, birth exists on the edge
Of extinction.

The heir, arriving tactlessly early,
Retires till you finish dying. With you go
Archaic patterns of a home you will never
Come home to. Like an amputation, it will
Haunt you in the grave.

(printed 1978)

JENNIFER RANKIN

A man is following me . . .

A man is following me.

I hurry away from the tram-stop
straight into the street of laurel trees

I hear him close behind stepping faster
we crisscross the street together

I check the distance to the end
My school shoes ringing out too loud

I feel his shadow in all the shadows
I feel his faltering

A man is following me
and I am getting to know him

all my life I have moved with his shadow
pacing the street in this slow mad dance

(before 1979)

ELAINE FEINSTEIN

Calliope in the labour ward

she who has no love for women
married and housekeeping

now the bird notes begin
in the blood in the June morning
look how these ladies are
as little squeamish as
men in a great war

have come into their bodies
as their brain dwindles to
the silver circle on
eyelids under sun
and time opens
pain in the shallows to wave up and over them

grunting in gas and air
they sail to a
darkness without self
where no will reaches

in that abandon less
than human
give birth
bleak as a goddess

(printed 1977)

Phenomenal Woman

Pretty women wonder where my secret lies.
I'm not cute or built to suit a fashion model's size
But when I start to tell them,
They think I'm telling lies.
I say,
It's in the reach of my arms,
The span of my hips,
The stride of my step,
The curl of my lips.
I'm a woman
Phenomenally.
Phenomenal woman,
That's me.

I walk into a room
Just as cool as you please,
And to a man,
The fellows stand or
Fall down on their knees.
Then they swarm around me,
A hive of honey bees.
I say,
It's the fire in my eyes,
And the flash of my teeth,
The swing in my waist,
And the joy in my feet.
I'm a woman
Phenomenally.
Phenomenal woman,
That's me.

Men themselves have wondered
What they see in me.
They try so much
But they can't touch
My inner mystery.
When I try to show them
They say they still can't see.
I say,
It's in the arch of my back,
The sun of my smile,
The ride of my breasts,
The grace of my style.
I'm a woman
Phenomenally.
Phenomenal woman,
That's me.

Now you understand
Just why my head's not bowed.
I don't shout or jump about
Or have to talk real loud.
When you see me passing
It ought to make you proud.
I say,
It's in the click of my heels,
The bend of my hair,
The palm of my hand,
The need for my care.
'Cause I'm a woman
Phenomenally.
Phenomenal woman,
That's me.

(printed 1978)

Closed Order

The convent fronted the square, a pale façade
aloof to the noise and horses and crossings
of passionate feet. Bricked windows
were not supercilious, but final. Looking up,
there was wonder and fear in hearing it
said: a Closed order. We knew
that meant, they never came out, save dead.
Even lay servants carrying bread
were scanned through the Judas window
before the door opened a body's width,
and the bread carnal from the oven
cooled as it passed that dark sill.

Next door, we borrowed dimensions of silence,
order and closure alien to our living. Mute,
the question hung behind toys and dinners:
How do they do, with nothing of what we have?
How can they? How weird, dropping your own freedom
like cut hair, or papers blowing around the square.

One day at siesta I climbed
past drying sheets on the roof
up to the cistern and then
to the final tiles of the tower.
There was no space beyond the heat,
it impaled all colour and sound,
each horse in bridle and shafts,
the breath of the world was stopped;
when sudden and subtle, meridian broke
in raining notes, the patter of palms

and of strings: so I saw rustling
below and screened, on their roof, five nuns.
One played the guitar and four
were dancing sevillanas. Black habits fell
away from unorthodox arms and innocent smiles
met in incandescent pleasure.
Faces so pale, I had thought,
were supposed to be penitential.
Leaning, curving, they courted their sisters
with that dance, of the flesh, but in their order
they made it another thing.
The black skirts eddied and swirled
the glittering tiles of the floor, and the sun took up
their faces engraved in light.
For an hour, or two, or till night remade time,
I could not but watch, and even a boy
was ashamed to spy on such franchise.
Once down from the height I kept silent.

Years now, crossing other squares
and climbing up other towers, trying
to talk of freedom, and harder its finding,
I am still disturbed by that closed order
where, perfectly free, the daughters of God,
in open eye of the sun were calmly dancing.

(1978)

There is a Desert Here

I loved you in silence, without hope, jealous and afraid. – Pushkin

There is a desert here I cannot travel,
There is sand I cannot tip from my shoes.
Over my left eyebrow is a greenish bruise.
There is you, and there is me. I cannot choose
But love you, though you wrong me,
And make angry love to me, a smack
Like a caress, a careless move, and a crack
Appears in your loving, widening, widening.
It was a bad bargain I made with you.
Your green eyes and strutting maturity
Did not mix well with my long pale face
And my convent innocence, but they looked
At me, flashes of light, like sexual lightning,
Blackening my tree. At last I sprout
From the bole after all these years
When you might have thought my tears
Were gone, and my tortured tree was dead.

Come little creatures, walk on me,
Come little worms, slide upon me,
For no man will ever again.
I watched beetles and ladybirds
Long before you gathered birch twigs
To beat me in a field – in fun, of course,
And I will watch them again,
And grow old ungracefully, barefoot
And sluttish in my ways.

No more hauling of ashes,
I promise you.

(printed 1979)

The Sea Anemones

Grey mountains, sea and sky. Even the misty
seawind is grey. I walk on lichened rock
in a kind of late assessment, call it peace.
Then the anemones, scarlet, gouts of blood.
There is a word I need, and earth was speaking.
I cannot hear. These sea flowers are too bright.
Kneeling on rock, I touch them through cold water.
My fingers meet some hungering gentleness.
A newborn child's lips moved so at my breast.
I woke, once, with my palm across your mouth.
   The word is: *ever*. Why add salt to salt?
   Blood drop by drop among the rocks they shine.
   Anemos, wind. The spirit where it will.
Not flowers, no, animals that must eat or die.

(printed 1981)

LIZ LOCHHEAD

I Wouldn't Thank You for a Valentine

(*Rap*)
I wouldn't thank you for a Valentine.
I won't wake up early wondering if the postman's been.
Should 10 red-padded satin hearts arrive with a sticky
    sickly saccharine
Sentiments in very vulgar verses I wouldn't wonder if you
    meant them.
Two dozen anonymous Interflora roses?
I'd not bother to swither who sent them!
I wouldn't thank you for a Valentine.

Scrawl SWALK across the envelope
I'd just say 'Same Auld Story
I canny be bothered deciphering it –
I'm up to here with Amore!
The whole Valentine's Day Thing is trivial and commercial,
A cue for unleashing clichés and candyheart motifs to
    which I personally am not partial.'
Take more than singing telegrams, or pints of Chanel Five,
    or sweets,
To get me ordering oysters or ironing my black satin sheets.
I wouldn't thank you for a Valentine.

If you sent me a solitaire and promises solemn,
Took out an ad in the *Guardian* Personal Column
Saying something very soppy such as 'Who Loves Ya, Poo?
I'll tell you, I do, Fozzy Bear, that's who!'
You'd entirely fail to charm me, in fact I'd detest it
I wouldn't be eighteen for anything, I'm glad I'm past it.
I wouldn't thank you for a Valentine.

If you sent me a single orchid, or a pair of Janet Reger's in a
　　heart-shaped box and declared your Love Eternal
I'd say I'd not be caught dead in them they were politically
　　suspect and I'd rather something thermal.
If you hired a plane and blazed our love in a banner across
　　the skies;
If you bought me something flimsy in a flatteringly wrong
　　size;
If you sent me a postcard with three Xs and told me how you
　　felt
I wouldn't thank you, I'd melt.

　　(before 1985)

Stubborn

My Stone-Age self still scorns
attempts to prove us more
than upright animals
whose powerful skeletons
and sinewy muscled limbs
were made to be exhausted
by decades of labour
not subdued by thought,

despises still those dreamers
who forget, poets
who ignore, heroes
who defy mortality
while risking every failure,
spirits unsatisfied
by merely their own
bodily survival.

I know her awful strength.
I know how panic, envy,
self-defence, combine
with her tormented rage
because they will deny
her argument that nothing
but the body's pleasure,
use, and comfort, matters.

Guarding her cave and fire
and implements, stubborn
in her ignorance,
deaf to all refutation,

I know she must insist
until the hour of death
she cannot feel the pain
that shapes and haunts me.

(printed 1983)

ANNE STEVENSON

Bloody Bloody

Who I am? You tell me
first who you are,
that's manners. And don't shout.
I can hear perfectly well.

Oh. A psychologist.
So you think I'm mad.

Ah, just unhappy.

You must be stupid if you
think it's mad to be unhappy.
Is that what they teach you
at university these days?

I'm sure you're bloody clever.

Bloody? A useful word.
What would *you* say, jolly?

It's bloody bloody,
I assure you,
having to sit up
for a psychiatrist –
sorry, *behavioural psychologist*,
I know there's a difference –
when I want to
lie down and sleep.

The only sensible thing,
at my age, is to be
as well you know
dead, but since they

can't or won't manage
anything like that here,
I consider my right to sleep
to be bloody sacred.

I can't hear you,
I'm closing my eyes.

I said *keep the curtains shut*!

Thankyou.
                    Hate you?
Of course I hate you,
but I can't, in honesty,
say I blame you.
You have to do your job.

There.
That's my telephone.
How fortunate.
You'll avail yourself
of this opportunity, won't you,
to slip tactfully away.

Hello? Yes,
two pieces of good news.
One,
you've just interrupted a most
unnecessary visit,
a young psychological person
is seeing herself out.
Two,
you'll be relieved
to hear I'm worse, much worse.

To the Days

From you I want more than I've ever asked,
all of it – the newscasts' terrible stories
of life in my time, the knowing it's worse than that,
much worse – the knowing what it means to be lied to.

Fog in the mornings, hunger for clarity,
coffee and bread with sour plum jam.
Numbness of soul in placid neighbourhoods.
Lives ticking on as if.

A typewriter's torrent, suddenly still.
Blue soaking through fog, two dragonflies wheeling,
Acceptable levels of cruelty, steadily rising.
Whatever you bring in your hands, I need to see it.

Suddenly I understand the verb without tenses.
To smell another woman's hair, to taste her skin.
To know the bodies drifting underwater.
To be human, said Rosa – I can't teach you that.

A cat drinks from a bowl of marigolds – his moment.
Surely the love of life is never-ending,
the failure of nerve, a charred fuse?
I want more from you than I ever knew to ask.

Wild pink lilies erupting, tasseled stalks of corn
in the Mexican gardens, corn and roses.
Shortening days, strawberry fields in ferment
with tossed-aside, bruised fruit.

(1991)

Lullaby

Time to rest now; you have had
enough excitement for the time being.

Twilight, then early evening. Fireflies
in the room, flickering here and there, here and there,
and summer's deep sweetness filling the open window.

Don't think of these things anymore.
Listen to my breathing, your own breathing
like the fireflies, each small breath
a flare in which the world appears.

I've sung to you long enough in the summer night.
I'll win you over in the end; the world can't give you
this sustained vision.

You must be taught to love me. Human beings must be
    taught to love
silence and darkness.

(printed 1992)

CAROL ANN DUFFY

Valentine

Not a red rose or a satin heart.

I give you an onion.
It is a moon wrapped in brown paper.
It promises light
like the careful undressing of love.

Here.
It will blind you with tears
like a lover.
It will make your reflection
a wobbling photo of grief.

I am trying to be truthful.

Not a cute card or a kissogram.

I give you an onion.
Its fierce kiss will stay on your lips,
possessive and faithful
as we are,
for as long as we are.

Take it.
Its platinum loops shrink to a wedding-ring,
if you like.

Lethal.
Its scent will cling to your fingers,
cling to your knife.

(printed 1993)

Morning in the Burned House

In the burned house I am eating breakfast.
You understand: there is no house, there is no breakfast,
yet here I am.

The spoon which was melted scrapes against
the bowl which was melted also.
No one else is around.

Where have they gone to, brother and sister,
mother and father? Off along the shore,
perhaps. Their clothes are still on the hangers,

their dishes piled beside the sink,
which is beside the woodstove
with its grate and sooty kettle,

every detail clear,
tin cup and rippled mirror.
The day is bright and songless,

the lake is blue, the forest watchful.
In the east a bank of cloud
rises up silently like dark bread.

I can see the swirls in the oilcloth,
I can see the flaws in the glass,
those flares where the sun hits them.

I can't see my own arms and legs
or know if this is a trap or blessing,
finding myself back here, where everything

in this house has long been over,
kettle and mirror, spoon and bowl,
including my own body,

including the body I had then,
including the body I have now
as I sit at this morning table, alone and happy,

bare child's feet on the scorched floorboards
(I can almost see)
in my burning clothes, the thin green shorts

and grubby yellow T-shirt
holding my cindery, non-existent,
radiant flesh. Incandescent.

(printed 1995)

Acknowledgements

The editors and publishers gratefully acknowledge permission to reprint copyright material in this book as follows:

VALENTINE ACKLAND: from *The Nature of the Moment*, published by Chatto & Windus; used by permission The Random House Group Limited. FLEUR ADCOCK: from *Poems 1960–2000* (Bloodaxe, 2000), by permission of Bloodaxe Books Limited. MAYA ANGELOU: from *And Still I Rise* (Virago/Random House, 1978), copyright © 1978 by Maya Angelou: used by permission of Little Brown and Company, UK, and Random House, Inc. MARGARET ATWOOD: from *Morning in the Burned House*, copyright © 1995 by Margaret Atwood; reprinted by permission of Houghton Mifflin Company; all rights reserved. MARY BARNARD: from *Sappho: A New Translation* (University of California Press), copyright © 1958 The Regents of the University of California; © renewed 1986 Mary Barnard. ELIZABETH BARTLETT: from *A Lifetime of Dying: Poems 1942–1979* (Peterloo Poets, 1979). PATRICIA BEER: from *Collected Poems*, by permission of Carcanet Press. ELIZABETH BISHOP: FROM *The Complete Poems 1927–1979*, copyright © 1979, 1983 by Alice Helen Methfessel; reprinted by permission of Farrar, Straus & Giroux Inc. LOUISE BOGAN: from *The Blue Estuary: Poems 1923–1968* (The Ecco Presss, 1977). GWENDOLYN BROOKS: © Estate of Gwendolyn Brooks, c/o Third World Press. Gay Clifford: from *Poems by Gay Clifford* (Hamish Hamilton,1990). EMILY DICKINSON: reprinted by permission of the publishers and the Trustees of Amherst college from *The Poems of Emily Dickinson*, Thomas H. Johnson, ed., Cambridge, Mass: The Belknap Press of Harvard University Press, copyright © 1951,1955, 1979 by the President and Fellows of Harvard College. H.D. (Hilda Doolittle): from *Collected Poems*, by permission of Carcanet Press and New Directions. FREDA DOWNIE: from *Collected Poems*, edited by George Szirtes (Bloodaxe, 1995), by permission of Bloodaxe Books Limited. CAROL ANN DUFFY: from *Mean Time* (Anvil, 1993), by permission of Anvil Press. RUTH FAINLIGHT: from *Selected Poems* (Sinclair-Stevenson, 1995), reprinted by permission of the author.

U. A. FANTHORPE: from *Side Effects* (Peterloo, 1978). ELAINE FEINSTEIN: from *Selected Poems* (Carcanet, 1994), reproduced by permission of Carcanet Press. LOUISE GLÜCK: from *The Wild Iris*, by permission of Carcanet Press and Ecco Press. GWEN HARWOOD: from *The Lion's Bride* (Angus and Robertson, 1981). ELIZABETH JENNINGS: from *Collected Poems* (Carcanet, 1986), by permission of David Higham Associates Ltd. JENNY JOSEPH: from *Rose in the Afternoon and Other Poems* (J. M. Dent, 1974). MAXINE KUMIN: from *The Retrieval System* (Panguin, 1978). DENISE LEVERTOV: from *Poems 1960–1967*, copyright © 1966 by Denise Levertov; reprinted by permission of New Directions Publishing Corp. and Gerald Pollinger, Ltd. LIZ LOCHHEAD: from *True Confessions and New Clich³s* (Polygon Books, 1985). AUDRE LORDE: 'On a Night of the Full Moon' from *Collected Poems* by Audre Lorde, copyright © 1997 by the Estate of Audre Lorde; used by permission of W. W. Norton & Company, Inc. AMY LOWELL: from *The Complete Poetical Works of Amy Lowell*, copyright © 1955 Houghton Mifflin Company, copyright © renewed 1983 by Houghton Mifflin Company, Brinton P. Roberts, and G. D'Andelot Belin, Esquire; reprinted by permission of Houghton Mifflin Company; all rights reserved. CHARLOTTE MEW: from *Collected Poems and Selected Prose*, reproduced by permission of Carcanet Press, Ltd. ELMA MITCHELL: from *The Poor Man in the Flesh* (Peterloo, 1976). MARIANNE MOORE: from *Selected Poems* (Faber and Faber, 1969), by permission of Faber and Faber Limited. OODGEROO, of the tribe of Noonuccal: 'No More Boomerang' from *My People*, 3e, The Jacaranda Press, © 1990; reproduced by permission of John Wiley & Sons, Australia. DOROTHY PARKER: from *The Collected Dorothy Parker* (Gerald Duckworth, 1973). RUTH PITTER: from *Collected Poems*, reprinted by permission of Enitharmon Press. SYLVIA PLATH: from *Collected Poems* (Faber and Faber, 1981), © The Estate of Sylvia Plath, 1981, reproduced by permission of Faber and Faber Limited. KATHLEEN RAINE: from *The Collected Poems of Kathleen Raine* (Golgonooza Press, 2000). JENNIFER RANKIN: from *Collected Poems*, University of Queensland Press, 1990. ADRIENNE RICH: 'To the Days' from *Dark Fields of the Republic: Poems 1991–1995* by Adrienne Rich, copyright © Adrienne Rich, 1995; used by permission of the author and W. W. Norton & Co, Inc. MURIEL RUKEYSER: from *The Collected Poems of Muriel Rukeyser*, reprinted by permission of International Creative Management, Inc.; copyright © 1978, Muriel Rukeyser. VITA SACKVILLE WEST: from *Orchard and*

Index of Poets

Index of First Lines